BOSNIA
HOPE IN
THE ASHES

For Joanna —
another pilgrim
on the way —

August, 1998

ACKNOWLEDGEMENTS

A book such as this needs a lot of help, and this one got it. First, there was Milanka of 206 Tours in New York. She had been able to get me into Sarajevo in December 1991, just before the shooting began, and she came through again on this one.

Then there was Jeff Reed, whose indefatigable Ford Escort became a faithful friend.

And Dr. Peter Kuzmic of Gordon-Conwell Theological Seminary and the Evangelical Theological Seminary of Osijek, who opened doors no one else could.

And Alitalia, for their most gracious hospitality.

And a relay team of transcribers—Janet Edmonson, Betty Murray, and Jackie Hempel—who turned twenty-seven hours of tape into several hundred pages of raw material.

And Betty Pugsley, who believed I could do it, when I did not.

And finally, Lonnie Hull DuPont, an editor *nonpareil*, who knew how to bring out the book that was there.

Blessed are

the peacemakers:

for they shall be called

the children of God.

—Matthew 5:9

TABLE OF CONTENTS

Pronouncing Guide

Here are some Bosnian names mentioned in this book, with my best attempt at rendering them in recognizable syllables.

Beslagic	Bes-*lahdg*-itch
Bijelo	*Bee*-yel-o
Brijeg	*Bree*-yay
Capljina	Cap-*lyeen*-a
Doboj	*Doe*-boy
Gasinci	*Gahz*-in-tsee
Grbavica	Grr-bah-*veetz*-a
Hercegovina	Her-tzeh-*go*-vinna
Jablanica	Yah-*blah*-neetz-a
Janja	*Yahn*-yah
Jasmina	Yahz-*meen*-a
Konjic	*Kone*-yeetz
Kraljeva	*Krahl*-yeh-va
Kraljevic	*Krahl*-yeh-vich
Ljubuski	Lyou-*bush*-key
Makjenovac	Mahk-*yen*-ovac
Medjugorje	Med-jew-*gor*-yay
Osijek	O-see-yek
Pale	*Pah*-lay
Podbrdo	*Pod*-brr-doe
Polje	*Pole*-yay
Selim	Sell-*eem*
Skrinjaric	*Screen*-yar-itch
Sutjeska	Soo-*shyets*-ka
Thibor	*Tee*-bor
Ustase	*Oo*-sta-shay
Vares	*Vahr*-esh
Vlajic	*Vlah*-tzik
Vukovar	*Voo*-ko-var

FOREWORD

If you're like me, Bosnia has been an incomprehensible muddle. A kaleidoscope of horrifying news, images of mass murder of civilians, wholesale raping of women and girls, and mindless shelling of defenseless cities. All seemed to be a result of geographic and religious factions raging against each other. And a new term came into being: "ethnic cleansing."

What was going on? What did it all mean? And is there any hope at all? If you wondered too, then this book is for you. For in following David Manuel on his perilous journey through the labyrinth of Bosnia, you'll not only begin to understand the complexities of its turmoil, but you will be heartened by the realization that there is real hope for peace.

But it will not come through the presence of NATO's "peacekeepers," air power and heavy tanks. As you travel with the author, you will meet the real peacemakers: selfless, dedicated individuals leading their lives on behalf of all peoples there, no matter what ethnic group or religion. It is their examples which will turn the tide.

You will meet Father Svet, an indefatigable priest with the audacity of an Arnold Schwarzenegger hero, the spirit of Joan of Arc, and the humor of Jay Leno.

Nikola and Sandra, a young couple who, working

through their church, reach out to Serbs, Muslims, and Croats alike.

A heroic mayor calls the bluff of an enemy commander ready to shell his town.

A Muslim woman, in terrible crisis, sees Christ in the lives of others and changes her life so completely that even in her own turmoil, she is able to help her neighbors.

And there are many more of these little-known heroes—graphic witnesses when we realize that Bosnia is a microcosm of our world today. The same flames of racial hatred flare in our cities. The same "it's payback time" syndrome can be heard in the Oklahoma City explosion and other bombings. The brutal imposition of force is echoed in our military sex scandals. And the slurs of prejudice slither across polished boardroom tables.

No constitutional law or cop on the beat or remote television security camera can effectively prevent the above, anymore than military might can bring about a permanent peace in Bosnia.

It will take individuals like those heroes in Bosnia, unnamed and unsung, to win the battle between light and darkness. And that means you and me.

You will take two journeys in this book. One physically down war-torn roads in Bosnia, the other spiritually through the author. Fasten your seatbelt for the ride of your life.

Richard Schneider
Senior Staff Editor
Guideposts
New York

PROLOGUE

I did not want to go back to Bosnia in 1996. I had visited that country four times in the four years prior to the recent war there and once during it. I had grown to love that country with its raw, jagged mountains and down-to-earth people. I wanted to remember her the way she had been and would never be again.

Bosnia was a place where one made friends quickly, if one were going to make them at all. The people had lived hard lives: under the Ottoman Turks for four centuries, then the Austro-Hungarians, then the Nazis during World War II, followed by forty-three years under Communism. When democracy finally arrived, they were not quite sure how to greet it. As with each stranger, they took their time assessing it.

The people of Bosnia would meet a stranger halfway. If they liked his or her heart, they would open their own. If his friendship proved reliable, gradually they would come to trust him. But they were careful; they had been burned many times.

I had made a few life-friends over there, including a mountain priest who had received his first pair of shoes when he was six and a nun who had more courage than I could ever hope to possess. It's funny how a few people can color a whole country for you; I liked the color of Bosnia and had no desire to see how it had changed. That memory-drawer could remain shut; why add a new file of horror and devastation?

So when Paraclete Press approached me in the spring of 1996 to go back again, I was inclined to say no. I had already done three book collaborations for them, focused on the apparitions of the Virgin Mary in the remote mountain village of Medjugorje in Bosnia's southernmost sector. And just before the war in neighboring Croatia spilled over into that little republic, I had done a brief history of the region and an update on the phenomenon still occurring in the little village with the unpronounceable name.

As I explained to Paraclete, I was several years behind on the promised delivery of a book to another house, and my publisher's smile, though still in place, was getting a bit thin. Besides, a number of exceptional books on the situation on Bosnia had already appeared,[1] and it seemed as if nothing new needed to be added.

But Paraclete wanted a different type of book, one that would look into the heart of Bosnia and see what role faith had played—or not played—during the long nightmare from which her people were only now awakening. They wanted a book that would take in all of Bosnia, not just Medjugorje and Mostar, a book that would reflect the hearts of Serbs and Muslims as well as Croats.

---

[1] Among them: Misha Glenny, central European correspondent for the BBC's World Service, had written a highly acclaimed personal account (*The Fall of Yugoslavia*, Penguin Books, 1993). Laura Silber, Balkan correspondent for London's *Financial Times*, and Allan Little of the BBC had co-authored a book to accompany the superb television documentary series (*Yugoslavia: Death of a Nation*, TV Books, 1996). And on this side of the Atlantic the searing war diary of Washington Post correspondent, Peter Maass, who told it all and got it all right (*Love Thy Neighbor*, Knopf, 1996).

As I weighed the assignment, it came to me that as far as eternity was concerned, there were no sides to the recent conflict; there was only tragedy. At present an immense bitterness pervaded the country. All sides had suffered atrocities the likes of which, according to the media, had not been seen since World War II. My own sources there informed me that these atrocities were beyond human imagining.

For the moment, there was peace, imposed by a massive array of NATO armament. But because of all that had been done during the war, expert opinion concurred that if the foreign troops were to pull out, the war-makers would have their way. The killing would resume, but worse than before. For this time there would be no one to intervene. The war-makers could play their murderous winner-take-all game until they were finally sated.

But what of the peacemakers? The war-makers were garnering all the headlines and the media attention they craved, as they called on their factions to harden their hearts. But what of the men and women whose hearts had somehow remained soft through all that had been done to them? What of the people who were now attempting to knit back together what humankind had torn asunder? Low-profile peacemakers—did they even exist?

I thought I knew of one or two and began to wonder if others might exist. Because if they did, then there might be hope for Bosnia after all.

The more I thought about it, the more intrigued I became, until finally I had to go, to find out for myself.

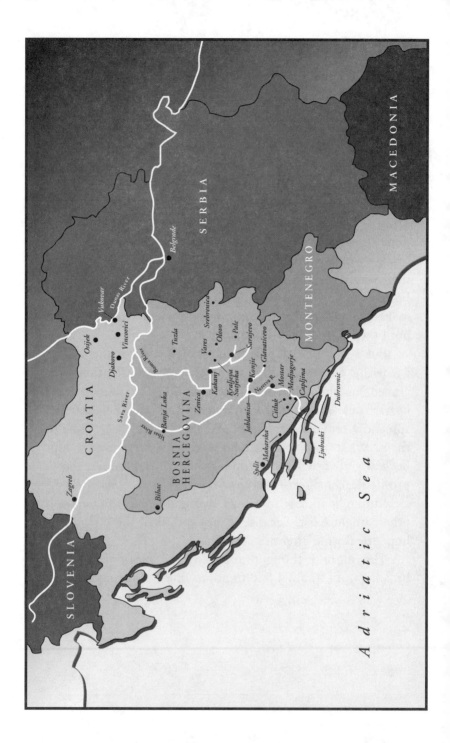

NIGHT FLIGHT

It was a Saint-Exupéry night. Somewhere to the plane's left hung a quarter moon—not enough to fade the points of icy brilliance across the night sky. Not a cloud appeared beneath us; it was actually possible to see the surface of the ocean far below, glistening like a wet black slate. Almost imperceptibly the big plane banked a few degrees to the left, then resumed course. During the maneuver, I caught a glimpse of why: ahead of us on the right was a cumulus build-up. In the pale moonlight it had substance—a shimmering white tower, reaching up almost to the plane.

Saint-Exupéry would have loved this night. It was easy to imagine him about twenty thousand feet lower, piloting his tiny aeroplane between immense cloud formations like the one ahead. The first of the poet-aviators, he had flown the mail across the Atlantic in the late 1930s and had written several volumes about his beloved obsession. Millions loved him for *The Little Prince*; I loved him for *Night Flight* and *Wind, Sand, and Stars*. He died during World War II, shot down on a reconnaissance mission over the Mediterranean.

Discovering Saint-Exupéry in college, I immediately added him to my list of favorite writers—Hemingway,

Fitzgerald, Faulkner, Nabokov, Shaw (Irwin, not George Bernard), Greene, Waugh, O'Hara, Steinbeck—hopeless romantics all. I was determined to become one of them.

The plane sailed on through the night. Everyone else in the darkened cabin was asleep; even the flight attendants, I suspected, were dozing. There were still three hours before a sleepy but smiling crew would begin serving breakfast to sleepy, unsmiling passengers prior to our descent into Rome. I had tried to sleep, but my mind kept ticking over, imagining figures in leather flying suits and white silk scarves, brave men and women in fragile machines. Saint-Exupéry was the first to write about flying, but he was not the best. The best was Beryl Markham, the girl who stole Denys Finch-Hatton from Isak Dinesen. She was the first woman to solo across the Atlantic, and she did it the hard way, flying into the prevailing westerlies. Coming down on Cape Breton Island, she managed to dump her plane on its nose. But she could write better than she could land; after reading *West with the Night*, Hemingway had said she was the best of all of them, and he might be right.

I had done some flying myself after college. On the ferry to Newport, Rhode Island, on my way to the Naval Officer Candidate School, I got seasick and realized I might be in for an exceedingly unpleasant three years. Instead, I became an airborne CIC officer and navigator and logged 2,600 hours flight time out of Newfoundland and Iceland. Some of it had been on nights like this, and they never ceased to grip me.

Finding that I also got airsick (the one advantage to flying was that you passed through the storms more quickly), I never pursued a pilot's license. Instead, when I got out of the navy I pursued a career in publishing, figuring that if I couldn't write the Great American Novel, the next best thing was to discover the one who was going to. But New York was not hiring editors without experience. I was about to try advertising, when my last trump card came through.

An editor at Doubleday, Coby Britton, had also been editor of the Yale Lit and had published more of my stories than anyone else's. When I called him, he told me of an opening in their copywriting department and put in a word for me. For two years I wrote dust-jacket copy. It paid next to nothing, but it was the best internship a writer or editor could have. In six hundred words or less you had to persuade a browser to part with $7.95 (top dollar for hardcovers in those days).

Editors began requesting that I be assigned to do their flap copy, and I began requesting that I be assigned to the editorial department. The break came when I was given a chance to line-edit a Doubleday author's second novel which was about to be rejected. The salvage job worked; the book was made into a movie, and I was given the job of assistant to the editor-in-chief.

Bachelor life in New York lived up to my Algonquin-round-table expectations. In fact, all of life was a novel. The only problem was, whoever was writing it seemed to have a wry and sometimes cynical sense of humor. As a hopeless romantic, I was in love with love and therefore most of the time wretchedly unhappy. If it was true that writers must first suffer, then I was certainly getting ready. Fortunately the tall, willowy, would-be actress (and hopeless romantic) to whom I kept proposing kept saying no. I finally met and married someone exactly my opposite, imbued with much common-sense wisdom. But in one area we were exactly alike: we shared the same sense of humor.

After a three-year stint in Toronto as Doubleday Canada's first editor, I returned to the New York office as the youngest editor, commuting from our home in Princeton.

Our marriage was not in good shape. Communication, its linchpin, had broken down, and as for humor, it had been months since we had laughed together. The only thing that held us together was our parents' strong disapproval of divorce, but even that bond was dissolving.

Then something extraordinary happened. I was working on a book by a man who had hooked up a lie detector to a plant and obtained a readout. Apparently the plant (a rhododendron) was responding to its environment on a subemotional level. The man's name was Cleve Baxter, and the Baxter Effect had been replicated in some highly reputable labs, as well as being written up in *Science*. The project had best-seller written all over it.

One day, the author, giving a talk at Wainwright House in Rye, New York, confided to an audience of blue-haired ladies in tennis shoes that he and his associates had recently figured out a way to measure the response of a *rock* and had obtained a muted readout; even the rock, it seemed, was responsive to its environment. Delighted at the audience's collective gasp, Baxter chuckled: "Science has no explanation for this."

At that moment the thought came to me: *That is because the answer is too simple for science. The plant, the rock— everything—has a common denominator: they were all created by the same hand.*

I sat there, stunned. Where did *that* come from? But there was no question about the conclusion my intellect was now making: God was real.

Now I was more than stunned. Many times in college I had stayed up all night arguing philosophy, yet had anyone ever suggested the reality of a personal deity, I would have laughed in his face. And probably quoted Marx to him, about religion being the opiate of the masses. But now. . . .

I got up and left the room and found a library where I could be alone. God was real? Well, I did have the strange feeling I was not alone. In fact, I felt bathed in invisible sunlight.

Then the thought came to my heart: *You will never be lonely again.*

I was surprised at that; I made friends easily and had lots of them. Good friends. But my heart reminded me how desperately lonely I had felt, even surrounded by friends.

Another thought came: *You need never be afraid again.* That, too, was a surprise: I did not think of myself as a fearful person. I had done skydiving, downhill ski-racing—but then my heart reminded me of all the things I was afraid of: the future, failure, rejection, not living up to my father's expectations.

The next thought was the biggest surprise of all: *You can stop despising yourself.* Most of the time my problem was arrogance. My heart explained that it was mainly to cover my inner conviction that I was really a superficial person, no more than a dilettante.

This sort of rolling revelation went on for quite a while, and with each new insight, another weight was lifted from the sack I had been carrying over my shoulder. I felt pretty light by the end of the evening.

And the next morning, the lightness had not dissipated. Not only was God real, I realized, but apparently He had been waiting all my life for me to realize it. And He loved me, beyond all human comprehension. I was dumbfounded.

But when I tried to tell my wife, Barbara, what had happened to me, I made a mess of it. The only thing of which I managed to convince her was that I had finally gone over the edge. I was sad about that but not dejected, because now there was hope for us. Someone else was in the equation now, and He was not going to let our marriage be torn asunder.

Barbara was sure I had gone completely crazy when I came home from work and announced that, after eight fast-track years at Doubleday and a bright future, I had just quit my job. But when I told her that I had decided to try the other side of the desk, she stuck by me. Three months later I was researching a book on Christian communities, and the following spring at a married-couples retreat at such a community on Cape Cod, she made the same vertical connection I had—a year to the day after my own conversion experience. I spent that summer at the community, gathering material for the book, and she and our daughter Blair joined me for a month, then another and another. At the end of the summer, we became members.

That was twenty-five years ago. We are still there. I never did write the Great American Novel, but I did write other books, about one a year, the majority of them collaborations. I would spend a week or two with people who had a story to tell, interviewing them constantly. Then working from transcripts, I would fashion a book for them. The job usually took four or five months. The one in 1988 took a year, but it became a top-of-the-list best-seller and was the project that introduced me to Bosnia.

A flight attendant came down the aisle. Seeing I was still awake, she asked if I would like to see the second movie. I shook my head; I was more interested in seeing where these recollections were going.

Bosnia-Hercegovina—I had never heard of it, until I collaborated on the last book by the late David du Plessis.[2]

---

[2] *Simple & Profound*, Paraclete Press, 1986.

Time magazine had called David the father of the modern Pentecostal movement and one of the seven spiritual giants of our age. He was a key member of the ongoing Catholic-Protestant dialogue and a dear friend of John Paul II. I knew him as the most humble man I had ever met.

In 1984, three years after the apparitions of the Virgin Mary had begun appearing daily to six young children in a remote mountain village called Medjugorje in the Yugoslav republic of Bosnia-Hercegovina, David, at the request of Yugoslavia's Cardinal Kuharic, had gone to the village to assess the phenomenon. With him was a young pastor from Osijek in eastern Croatia, acting as his interpreter and guide. As David put it, he went as a "fruit inspector." When discerning whether something supernatural was of God, or a masterful deception by the Angel of Light, there was one sure test, the one Jesus had outlined to his followers on a hillside in Galilee. "A good tree cannot bring forth evil fruit, neither can a corrupt tree bring forth good fruit. . . . Wherefore, by their fruits ye shall know them" (Matt 7:18, 20).

David came away from his visit convinced that what was happening in Medjugorje was of God. And he had urged me to go there. But my anti-Catholic bias was far stronger than his, and besides I had other books to write.

In 1987, my wife had gone to Medjugorje with a few others from home. She had begged me to come, too, but again I was too busy. I had to admit, however, that her visit to the village had a profound effect on her. After she returned, the first noticeable change occurred in her morning routine. Before, no one disturbed her until she'd had two cups of coffee and finished the crossword; then she was open for business. Now she skipped the coffee and puzzle, using that time for prayer and devotional reading in our bedroom, which I was invited out of.

Her spiritual life began to deepen, until doing God's will was the only thing that mattered to her. Of course, ever since my conversion I had said the same thing. But as the old prayer book put it, it was on my lips, but not in my life. Now, when I complained about something, Barbara would ask me, "Do you think it's God's will?"

"Well, I suppose so, but—"

She would shrug. "If it's God's will, then do it."

"But I don't feel like—"

"Then ask Him to change your heart."

In 1988 she told me of a Protestant newspaper publisher named Wayne Weible in South Carolina who had written some wonderful columns about Medjugorje. He had been asked for copies so often, he finally collected them into a tabloid, of which there were now twelve million copies in print. For two years he had been trying to write a book, but he had not gotten it off the ground. Since part of my call was to help people put their stories into book form, why didn't I offer to help him?

"Look," I replied testily, "Medjugorje is your thing, not mine. I've got plenty on my plate as it is, and besides—"

"Why don't you ask Him?"

"Who?"

"God."

So I did. And then I wrote to Wayne Weible, who was initially as averse to the idea as I had been. But we met and talked, and two weeks later at the end of May 1988, we were on our way.

Wayne and I landed in Belgrade, the capital of Yugoslavia. The country was Communist then, but that did not explain why the officers at customs and passport control were so deliberately slow, cold, and rude. When I commented on them to Wayne, he explained that it was because we were going to

Medjugorje. In the seven years since the apparitions had begun, millions of pilgrims had visited there. Yet according to Communism, God did not exist. So anyone going to Medjugorje was a self-deluded fool, toward whom a good Communist could feel nothing but contempt.

Wayne told of helicopters buzzing the church during Mass and police forbidding outside gatherings. But lately, he added, the Communists, at least the local variety, were beginning to change their tune. They could see the influx of hard foreign currency. And so, like practically everyone else in the village, they began constructing new tourist accommodations and additions to their homes. You could tell which ones were Communists, Wayne said smiling; they were the ones who kept working even though it was Sunday.

From Belgrade, we flew to Mostar, capital of Hercegovina, the lower province of the republic whose full name was Bosnia-Hercegovina but which everyone simply called Bosnia. Judging from the large number of gray-green helicopters and troop transports, the airport was primarily a military base, where the JNA (the Yugoslav National Army) had a sizable contingent. Even so, the attitude of the people behind the counters was noticeably warmer.

We hired a cab and soon began to climb up out of the Neretva River valley. By now it was late afternoon, and the slanting sun softened the rock outcroppings which were everywhere. It made the valley below seem an idyllic patchwork of neatly edged fields bordered by stone walls. The valley was broad, flat, and fertile. Most of the soil in Bosnia was not rich, and often little of it covered the rocky substrata, but the farmers made the most of every acre. Up north, in the province of Bosnia, the urban areas were fairly industrialized, especially around Zenica, Tuzla, and Sarajevo (capital of both that province and all Bosnia-Hercegovina).

But down here in the south it was still largely agricultural. Here the population was mostly Croatian, while up north it was mostly Muslim, and to the east, mostly Serbian.

Looking down in the valley, I was struck by how peaceful it seemed, in spite of all the military hardware we had seen parked at the airport. I imagined it looked pretty much the way it had when Cyril and Methodius had come here eleven hundred years ago. The roads were paved now, but they were few in number, they were not wide, and they were almost empty.

All at once I felt awfully glad to be here.

The driver hugged the side of the mountain as a big truck came around the corner and swept past us. I wondered what would have happened had we been a truck as big as that one. There were no guardrails on this road, and the corners were either blind or tight switchbacks. As we rounded the next one, I peered down a thousand feet and spied rusted wrecks of cars which had not made it.

Finally we were up on the plateau—barren save for windswept scrub pines. Occasionally we would see a few goats or a bit of soil where someone had managed to grow a few beans. It was hardscrabble land. We passed through the hamlet of Milakovici: a scattering of two- and three-room houses of white stucco with red tile roofs. Wood was at a premium here, but red clay was in abundance.

Next came Citluk: tree-shaded, tan buildings, some shops, some cars—a small but bustling town. And then we turned on the road to Medjugorje. Wayne grinned with anticipation. It was as if he were returning home, which in a way he was; this was his eighth trip back. The main street, if you could call it that, was a narrow paved road with a few shops on it and with a large church waiting at the end. Its twin spires were aglow in the last rays of sun as we arrived.

We slipped inside the massive wooden doors; evening Mass had just begun. In the morning, Wayne whispered, there were Masses in Italian, English, and German for the pilgrims. This one, in Bosnian[3], was primarily for the villagers, though now the church was packed with pilgrims as well. The pews could hold 1,500 people, but probably twice that number were standing at the back, along the walls, and in the aisles.

I thought I recognized the hymn they were singing. The words were Bosnian, but the melody was—no, it couldn't be! I whispered to Wayne, "That can't be the 'Battle Hymn of the Republic'?"

He smiled and nodded. "It's one of her favorites."

"Whose?"

"The *Gospa's.*"

"*Whose?*"

"That's what they call the Virgin Mary."

Weird, I thought. *Definitely weird.*

More people were pressing in behind us, and I was separated from Wayne. I was standing in the center aisle, and there were so many people I could scarcely move. As the service continued, I caught a few nationality clues. The couple in front of me seemed to be French; the two women on my left were Italian. Next to them was a family apparently from the Philippines. And behind me were some students from Germany.

I felt a downward tug on the right sleeve of my windbreaker. I turned, and there, sitting at the end of the pew, was an old woman, all in black from her shoes to her babushka. Her hair was white, and her face was seamed

---

[3] Technically they were speaking what many used to call Serbo-Croatian. The Croats would insist it was Croatian; the Serbs, of course, spoke only Serbian. And the Muslims would say it was neither. For this book we will simply call it Bosnian.

with care. She must have been in her eighties. I couldn't figure out what she wanted. She tugged again on my sleeve and with her other hand pointed to her seat. She wanted me to take her seat.

Shocked, I frowned and shook my head. But she would not let go of my sleeve and kept tugging insistently. Not wanting to make a scene, I exchanged places with her. Now she was standing in the aisle, and I was sitting in her place. A flood of feelings and memories came over me. When I was little, riding on the Rapid Transit in Cleveland, my mother had always made me give my seat to any woman who needed one, and many of them had looked just like this woman. Thereafter, I always gave up my seat—until I lived in New York, where no one did so.

The Mass had come to the celebration of the Eucharist. With great difficulty the old woman got down on her knees on the stones of the aisle, while I knelt on her kneeler. Looking at her, I remembered something Wayne had told me: when the *Gospa* first had come in 1981, she had told the villagers that pilgrims would be coming, and that they were to open their homes to them and give to them, as if each pilgrim were her Son. This woman had nothing to give but her seat, and she gave that.

Tears came to my eyes. I looked around, until I found an old nun and motioned to her to take my place, which she gratefully did.

After the service we went to the home where we would be staying. Like most houses in Bosnia, it was one story with a corridor down the middle and a bathroom at the back. In the front of the house was a room which served as living and dining room, with a tiny kitchen off of it. We were in a small room at the end of the corridor with two beds in it. There were two other doors off the corridor which were always kept closed; I assumed they were the family's bedrooms. Having been up for thirty hours, we went to bed early.

The next morning, we went up Podbrdo, the hill on which the apparition first appeared. There was a steel cross there, at the base of which were the stubs of hundreds of candles. A slight breeze blew, and lavender thistles grew in tiny crevices, where no flower could possibly survive. It was exceptionally peaceful. I was growing to like this country quite a lot, though I had no particular reason to.

It was time to leave for the English Mass, so we went down and took a footpath through the fields. It had rained during the night, and the red dirt was still soft. It bore a record of the brands of the athletic shoes of the pilgrims who had passed that way: Adidas, Reebok, Nike. As we approached a vineyard, we heard a woman singing but could not see her. Then she emerged from the end of a row—an old woman with a pruning hook in her gnarled hand. She was crooning to the vines as she dressed them.

The English Mass might as well have been called the Irish Mass, for there were more Irish in attendance than English or Americans. Other than Croats, the first nationality to start coming had been the Italians, Wayne explained, then the Irish. By 1987, they were coming from all over. The Americans had arrived late but were making up for lost time. At the altar were seventeen priests concelebrating, all in white, all leading tours from their various homes. A shaft of morning sunlight came through the east window, illuminating the altar, reflecting off the white robes and white altar cloth. The whole area seemed to glow. It was not a long service, but time seemed suspended during it. I felt immense peace.

At breakfast we had made a couple of sandwiches of sliced salami and cheese and had tucked them into our windbreakers. Now, with a bottle of drinking water, we headed up Mount Krizevac. By American standards it was hardly a mountain, no more than fifteen hundred feet high. The boulders on the rocky path were worn smooth by millions of pairs of shoes, but the path was fairly steep in places and the climb took us over an hour. At the summit was a huge concrete cross erected in 1933, on the nineteen-hundredth anniversary of Christ's death. It could be seen for miles and was the reason why it was called Cross Mountain. Far below we could make out the village with all the red-roofed houses clustered about the church like chicks around a mother hen.

All over the summit were groups of pilgrims, praying or eating lunch. Those praying were saying the rosary, in Bosnian, English, French, Italian. Their prayers sounded like the soft hum of summer bees.

Late that afternoon, as we walked back through the fields, we stopped to watch an old farmer and his two sons forking hay onto a wagon with high staked sides. The wagon had rubber tires like a car's, but it was pulled by an old horse, which was contentedly grazing and waiting for them to finish. The forks they used were wooden with three prongs and could have been in the farmer's family for a hundred years.

The shadows were lengthening; everything was bathed in golden light that made the surroundings seem unreal. At the corner of the next field stood another old woman in black, with her grandson beside her. They offered us figs sprinkled with confectioner's sugar and a cup of water. We each took a fig. I tried to give the woman some money, but she smiled and shook her head.

As we walked away, Wayne explained that they had been told to give without expecting anything in return. He said that he had repeatedly tried to give money to the family with whom he stayed, but they would never accept it. They did like American coffee, though, so he always brought a couple of cans. I nodded and told him what I had seen that morning. One of the two doors which were always closed had been left slightly ajar. Inordinately curious, I looked in. It was a little bedroom, but in addition to the two beds there were two mattresses on the floor. Two members of that family were sleeping on the floor so that we could sleep in beds.

Every time I turned around, it seemed, I was freshly convicted of selfishness. Nobody ever said anything; they didn't have to. My heart got the message. I never did see anything supernatural (other than an entire village going to church every day). But at the end of the week I realized that I had never done so much thinking about God and my relationship to Him.

I loved the village now, as my wife did, and as did practically everyone else who had come here. And when it came time to go, I didn't want to leave. My desire to stay made no sense; everyone I loved, my work, and all my commitments were back on Cape Cod, halfway round the world. Yet I could not remember ever being so reluctant to leave a place. When I mentioned it to Wayne, he said, "Someone called this place the edge of heaven. You get a little foretaste of what heaven might be like, and though your head tells you that you have to go home, your heart doesn't want to leave."

I nodded. Now I understood why Barbara protected her morning quiet time as a lioness would her cubs. She had taken Medjugorje home with her.

I knew that I would return.

GLAVATICEVO

For the benefit of those still asleep, the cabin lighting was minimal. But along the edge of the pulled-down shade, a thin line of fire signaled that day was dawning out there. Seeing I was awake, a yawning flight attendant asked me if I cared for orange juice or coffee. I shook my head and asked her how much longer to Rome. Two hours. Suddenly I felt bone weary and closed my eyes. But my mind would not stop turning. Since I was on my way back to Bosnia—postwar Bosnia—it seemed urgent to recall prewar Bosnia. Right now I was recalling Glavaticevo.

That hidden mountain valley might have been the most beautiful place in all of Bosnia. It was a small, round valley, completely rimmed by old, grass-covered mountains, so high up that the Neretva River, which flowed through it, was little more than a fast-running stream. I particularly remembered one early morning when the valley was like a bowl full of mist. When the sun came up over the eastern rim, it could not penetrate the mist and was not yet high enough to burn it off. Instead, it made everything glow. Nearby leaves seemed iridescent. A chalet-style farmhouse with its steep red roof and tidy vegetable-garden glistened. The air was still, and so was everything else—even the valley's roosters who had greeted the coming dawn an hour before. Nothing moved. I took it all in, and it still occupied a double-page spread in my memory book.

I had gone there in the summer of 1991, to finish a collaboration with Svetozar Kraljevic, a Franciscan priest born and raised in the mountains of Hercegovina.[4] I had met Father Svet in Medjugorje three summers before. He was in his late thirties, slight of build, with a bald head and a nose like a hawk's. His most distinguishing feature was his gray eyes—sometimes sad, often alight with mischief, always full of compassion. Father Svet loved to tease, and his sense of humor was quick. But it was usually directed at himself; he was the only person I knew whose teasing never hurt. Mention his name to anyone who knew him, and an instant smile would be the response. When I first met him, I had the distinct impression: *Here is a surrendered life; learn from it.*

For two years I had begged Father Svet to let me help him tell his story, but he had steadfastly refused. "The work is what is important," he would say, "not the man doing the work. When one man leaves, another takes his place." But finally he relented, and during his next trip to the States as a spokesman for what God was doing in Medjugorje, I began the interviewing process with him.

By the summer of 1991, it was time for the two of us to go through the manuscript line by line, so that everything would be said exactly the way he wanted it, and the book would be his. That meant it was time for me to go to Bosnia— which would be a little tricky, since the day before I was scheduled to leave, the Serbian-controlled JNA had attacked the Republic of Slovenia for declaring its independence from

---

[4] *Pilgrimage*, Paraclete Press, 1991.

former Yugoslavia. With the collapse of Communism, the six republics of Yugoslavia, as elsewhere in the East Bloc, each held a referendum, asking their people to confirm the leadership they wanted. The only republics to remain Communist were Serbia and little Montenegro, but they promptly declared that they were still Yugoslavia; any republics like Slovenia and Croatia who declared their intent to break off from them would be forced by the JNA to rejoin.

With all of former Yugoslavia now a potential war zone, the U.S. ambassador in Belgrade strongly advised all American citizens to leave at once, while at home the State Department issued an equally strong advisory: Anyone who might be considering going to former Yugoslavia should reconsider. As if by confirmation, the night before I was due to leave, the lead story on the evening news showed JNA jets screaming down on Slovenian militia troops who were shooting back with old rifles.

My wife turned from the television screen and asked me quietly, "You're not seriously thinking of going into that, are you?"

I shrugged. "I'll admit it doesn't make a lot of sense. But I can't finish the project without Father Svet, and obviously he can't get out."

I agreed to call him to see how things were, which was easier said than done. Only a few trunk lines were open into former Yugoslavia, and all of them were tied up by American Slovenes frantic to know if their kin were all right. So I placed the call at 3:00 A.M., my time, and was able to get through to Father Svet. He was stationed in the monastery at Konjic on the Neretva River, about halfway from Mostar to Sarajevo.

He said that the fighting was more than two hundred

miles to the northwest as the crow flew. (That did not seem like much distance, until I remembered how many mountain ranges the crow would have to negotiate in former Yugoslavia; two hundred miles there were more like a thousand at home.) What was the worst-case scenario? The war might expand into eastern Croatia, Father Svet acknowledged, but that was still more than a hundred miles north. Then, as if he could see my crow soaring and diving through the mountains, he added, "It takes most of a day to drive from there to here." The clincher was that while Slovenia and Croatia had declared their independence, Bosnia had not (yet); technically it was still part of the rump state of Yugoslavia. The JNA might have infested Bosnia, but there was no reason for them to attack it.

That was enough assurance for me; I left the following afternoon. My friends thought I was either brave or crazy, probably mostly the latter. I didn't think I was either; it just felt right. And for some reason, I was not scared.

I flew PanAm to Dubrovnik, rented the fastest car the little agency had (an Opel), and started north, heading up the Neretva River valley. It was about five hours to Konjic, and the sun was setting by the time I reached the steepest and most spectacular part of the gorge. Running alongside the frothing river, it was an excellent road, the best in Bosnia, with broad sweeping bends and graceful free-form concrete spans.

At sunset the river gorge became a magical place. To the west, with the sun now down behind the mountain, the river was in deep shadow; I had on the highbeams. But up ahead to the north, where the peaks were still covered with snow, the last rays of sun created a dazzling, fiery display. In my mind I could hear Grieg's "Hall of the Mountain King."

The best part came as the road passed the mouth of the

Vrbas River which fed into the Neretva at Jablanica. There, looking west, the tributary's gorge was all golden light and hazy outcroppings in silhouette. With that cascading liquid fire in the left foreground and the burnished crimson peaks ahead in the distance, it reminded me of the American Hudson River School of painting. Like those works, if this scene were on canvas in a gallery, viewers would have a hard time believing the scene could be real.

It was dark when I arrived at the monastery. Father Svet greeted me warmly and took me to the little room that would be mine for the next few days. It was austere: a window, a bed, a straight-backed chair, a desk, and a lamp. All I needed.

In the morning I had breakfast with the six brown-robed friars. The talk, all in Bosnian, was mostly about the war news. Sitting next to me, Father Svet at first tried to translate, but after a while said he would fill me in later. The conversation was light, but I sensed an underlying concern. At any moment the war could break out in Croatia, and these men were Croatian, as well as Franciscans.

For the next two days we worked at my laptop—Father Svet nodding or shaking his head, me saving or trying again. It was slow going and became even slower, as the heat and humidity rose. Konjic was experiencing a heat wave, and air-conditioning was a luxury one would not find in a monastery. Finally Father Svet decided we needed a change of scenery. Father Tomislav Pervan, who had been pastor of Medjugorje when I first went there and was now vice-provincial (second in command) in Mostar, was taking eight young men about to enter seminary on a retreat to the Franciscans' retreat house in Glavaticevo. We would join them.

The house sat high on a hill—a three-story, white stucco,

red roof, chalet-type building with many small rooms, each with its own window and plenty of fresh, cool, dry air. I worked at a wooden picnic table in the backyard garden, joined frequently by Father Svet, who now was nodding much more often than shaking his head.

It was fascinating to watch the mood of the young men change. When they came, they were in high gear, chattering about their interests back home, humming popular tunes. But gradually, as the tranquillity of Glavaticevo seeped into them, their revolutions per minute settled down to idle, and they began to absorb. They received no formal instruction while there, but they had Mass every morning and vespers every afternoon with much time for thought and prayer and devotional reading in between. Father Tomislav, round and ruddy of face, full of common sense and inclined to speak in rapid-fire bursts, was always available for questions and talk.

In the afternoons the young men would go for walks or play soccer. I knew how important basketball was to Bosnia, but I had not realized that soccer was its equal, until I saw five of the novices standing in a circle, heading the ball to one another, as we might chuck a football. One young man bounced a soccer ball on his upraised knee forty-eight times; he would have gone on longer, but the supper-bell rang.

One afternoon Father Tomislav and Father Svet took their charges (with me trailing) to the site of two mass graves where three Franciscan priests and thirty villagers were buried. They had been killed by Tito's *partizani* when the Communists took over the valley after the war. Why? Because they were Croats, and during the war many Croats had sided with the Nazis. These hadn't, but it didn't matter. But surely the priests had nothing to do with the war? No. Then why were they killed? Because they were Croats.

It was my first taste of the age-old Balkan custom: "pay-back time." It was sickening to think that people could be killed simply for being the wrong nationality. Then I remembered the saying from the American frontier: "The only good Injun is a dead Injun." I remembered the black lynchings and the Jew-baiting, and all the other ugly ethnic clashes in America's past and present. The Balkans did not have a corner on mindless violence.

Later I would learn how payback time worked. If a people were unable to protect themselves or stand up to their oppressors, if terrible atrocities were being done to them, and there was no one to help them or make the bad things stop, then their only friend was history. If they were willing to wait long enough, someday the pendulum would swing back. Then they could do unto others what had been done unto them.

Where did it all begin? Probably in the third century, when the Church in Rome had become Latinized. Until then, all Christians had worshiped in Greek, as the Eastern Church continued to do. In 305 the Emperor Diocletian divided the Roman Empire in half, with the dividing line going through the Balkan Peninsula. Present-day Slovenia, the western half of Croatia, and all of Bosnia-Hercegovina would remain in the Western Roman Empire; Serbia, Macedonia, and the eastern half of Montenegro would henceforth be governed from Byzantium, capital of the Eastern Roman Empire. After the Emperor Constantine converted to Christianity, he rebuilt Byzantium and in 330 rechristened it Constantinople. It now became the headquarters of the Eastern Church, which took on the name Orthodox, Greek for "right belief."

Over the centuries other differences developed. The Eastern Orthodox Church believed in a collegiality of leadership, after the example of the apostles. The Patriarchs (heads of the Church) of each Eastern Orthodox nation considered themselves to be brothers in the apostolate, with the Pope merely first among equals. The Roman Catholic Church maintained that, as Christ's vicar on earth in an unbroken succession since God gave Peter the keys to the kingdom, the Pope had absolute authority over all cardinals—and patriarchs. As regarding the Church's proper relationship with civil government, Rome believed in the functional separation of church and state, since the aims of the two were often opposed. Constantinople, however, regarded the state as the secular arm of God; even an evil state had God's authority. Therefore, with rare exception the Orthodox were able to reach accommodation with the state, while the Western Church was often in opposition.

There were cultural differences, as well. The Orthodox Church felt that in the presence of God, out of respect one should remain standing and not sit or kneel as the Church in Rome did. They accepted lay theologians, whereas the Catholics believed that only the ordained should be educated. The East allowed its lower clergy to marry; the West insisted all priests remain celibate.

As the differences grew more pronounced, each Church became convinced that it was the more pure and its doctrine the more correct, despite the greater wealth or influence of the other (jealousy being ever the handmaiden of pride). Periodic attempts at reconciliation were made, invariably marked by intractability on both sides.

In the ninth century two brothers from Thessalonika, Cyril and Methodius, undertook the Christianization of all the Slavic peoples who had been migrating over the Carpathian Mountains and down into the Balkan Peninsula. These were the Serbs and the Croats, for whom the brothers first invented a Slavic alphabet based on Greek letters, which in its final form would be called Cyrillic, then used it to translate the Bible. The Pope gave his blessing to their endeavors, and "Old Church Slavonic" became the liturgical language of all the Slavic Churches.

One would think that two peoples who arrived at the same time, lived in close proximity, spoke the same language, and worshiped the same God would be able to get along. But the dividing line was in place: East was East, and West was West. The Croats, mostly in the west, were aligned with Rome; the Serbs, mostly in the east, were aligned with Constantinople. The division between the two Churches deepened until each Church considered the other corrupt beyond redemption. In 1054 the Pope and the Patriarch excommunicated each other.

Another century and a half would pass, however, before either side committed a collective harm against the other so grievous that it deserved paying back. But then in 1204 a Crusader army suddenly turned on Constantinople—raping, murdering, pillaging. To this day the event has such resonance in Orthodox memory that a non-Orthodox, unfamiliar with history, would never dream that it had happened nearly eight centuries ago.

Ever since then, one side has been paying back the other every chance it had. In the fifteenth century it became a three-way affair when the Ottoman Turks extended their empire down into the Balkans. Now Islam was competing with Roman Catholicism and Orthodoxy for the minds and hearts of the unconverted, and many living in Bosnia became Muslims.

What Saki once said of Cyprus applies even more here: The Balkans produce more history than they can locally consume.

In this century the pendulum continued to swing. In 1918, at the end of World War I, a democracy actually existed: The State of the Slovenes, Croats, and Serbs. It lasted thirty-five days. Alexander, regent of Serbia, replaced it with The Kingdom of Serbs, Croats, and Slovenes, with himself as king. He dissolved the National Council (in Zagreb) and set up the National Assembly (in Belgrade). Eight years later, he declared a new royal dictatorship: Yugoslavia ("The Kingdom of the South Slavs"). His first order of business was the complete subjugation of the Croats, which he sought to accomplish with the state's security police, augmented by ultranationalists known as *Chetniks* ("freedom fighters"). As the police looked the other way, the Chetniks committed atrocities so horrendous they were forever seared into the collective memory of the Croats.

The Croats' payback time came during World War II, when Hitler shifted his focus from West to East. In exchange for the Croats' cooperation as he drove toward Russia, he would give them the thing they had dreamed of for a thousand years: their own homeland. It was an offer they could not refuse, and they made a pact with the devil.

At the time, the Croats had their own ultranationalist faction: the *Ustase* ("Stand up"). With them in charge of the new state, which took in part of Serbia and all of Bosnia-Hercegovina, it was payback time in spades. The Ustase began doing to the Serbs what the Chetniks had done to the Croats—and worse, for each time the hatred spiraled around again, it was amplified. The Ustase set up a Nazi-style death camp to which they shipped thousands of Serbs, Jews, and gypsies (as well as an increasing number of Croats who could no longer remain silent in the face of mounting evidence of Ustase atrocities).

By 1943 it was becoming increasingly clear that the

Thousand-Year Reich was going to last only about ten years. Croatian and Serbian antifascists joined the Communist *partizani*, or partisans, until there were some 300,000 men conducting guerrilla warfare against the retreating Germans. But Serb and Croat contingents, seeking to settle who would rule over postwar Yugoslavia, were soon shooting more bullets at each other than at the enemy. This put the Allies in a quandary: whom should they support? They decided that their first priority was to end the war as quickly as possible. That decision meant backing the partisans under Josip Broz, who called himself Tito, even if that was tantamount to consigning postwar Yugoslavia to the Communist camp.

The partisans, now enjoying full Allied support, received help in their hunt for former Ustase from the Chetniks, who knew exactly where to look. It was payback time once again, and the Chetniks widened the scope of their revenge to include any Croats who happened to be in their path, such as the unfortunate souls at Glavaticevo.

But Tito, once he had consolidated power, determined to put an end to all ethnic strife. "You are Communists!" he thundered. "Nothing else!" And he made it stick; anyone disobeying him went to prison. In 1967 he boasted in Belgrade, "For fifty generations going back fifteen hundred years, every generation has wasted its youth in war. No generation has escaped this devastation. But now the fifty-first will, for I, Tito, and Communism, have brought this enmity between our peoples to a close!"

But Tito was dead now, and so was Communism. Was the hatred also dead? Judging from what was now happening up north, it only had been sleeping. Each afternoon just before vespers the two Franciscans went out to Father Svet's Volkswagen to listen to the war news. They came back solemn. Serb paramilitaries had just destroyed a Croatian village near the border while the JNA had looked the other way.

On our last day at Glavaticevo, having completed our work, Father Svet announced he was taking the eight friar-novices mountain climbing, and I was to come. We drove in a couple of vans to the base of one of the surrounding mountains and started up the path. It was a gentle climb, but after twenty minutes I was thankful for the cycling I had done at home. The path wound upward through sun-dappled shade across cold, tumbling brooks that flung diamonds into the sunlight. Occasionally the path passed through an open field, where we had a breathtaking view and could see how far we had ascended.

About midmorning we came to a two-room house set half into the side of the mountain. There we were greeted by an old babushka with two teeth left in her smile. She leaned heavily on her stick as she bade us come inside, where she insisted on giving us refreshments, though she could not have had two dinars to rub together. She doted on Father Svet as if he were her son, and he in turn gave her his full attention, as if he had nothing else to do that day.

When it was time to go, he reached into the knapsack of one of the novices and gave her a sack of coffee beans. Her eyes filled, as she smiled and patted him on the back. As we left, he confided to me: "Do you know, it takes her three hours to walk down to church. And she does it every Sunday." I was beginning to think that these old babushkas were the soul of Bosnia.

Two hours later we reached two more houses, close together, where three generations farmed, kept goats, and now chopped firewood, for there was no work to be had in the valley. I tried to recall if I had ever been to a home that was inaccessible by car but was lived in year-round and could not think of any.

We were going to have lunch with these people. With long planks they set up two outdoor tables and benches. We had brought bread and cheese and sausage—enough for all. But not to be outgiven, they produced sliced cucumbers and onions and grilled pieces of chicken. Father Svet was beaming. At first I thought it was just that he was glad to have the book done and to be free for a little while from the concerns of the monastery and the war news. Then I remembered that he had grown up in the mountains with people like these.

He was home.

THREE

THE CALM

A flight attendant handed me a customs declaration. "You'll need to fill this out, if you have anything to declare. We'll be landing in an hour." Smiling, I closed my eyes and went back to Bosnia that summer of 1991.

When Father Svet and I had returned to the monastery at Konjic, I called PanAm to confirm my flight, only to find that there was no flight. With former Yugoslavia now a war zone and the war having spread to Croatia, PanAm had canceled all service to that region.

"But I've got a ticket!" I exclaimed, making an effort to remain civil. "What am I supposed to do?"

"I'm sorry, sir," the agent replied, sounding weary, harried, and as if she, too, were making an effort to remain civil, "Our last flight left yesterday."

"Is there anything else flying out of Dubrovnik?" (I still had to return the car.)

"I don't know, sir; I'm in Zagreb. You might try Croatian Air."

I did try Croatian Air. And they did have a flight. But it was full, and the waiting list was so long, they had closed it.

I was stranded. I began to wish I had not read Herman Wouk's classic, *War and Remembrance*; all I could think of was the Jastrow family who had tarried in Italy just a little too long at the beginning of World War II. When they did try to get out, it was too late; they wound up at Teresienstadt, with old professor Jastrow perishing in a gas chamber.

When I mentioned my predicament to Father Svet, he did not seem overly concerned. "You will get out," he nodded. "Tomorrow you go to Dubrovnik; tonight I will show you our new church."

After supper he took me up to the mission church on the outskirts of town, which he served as pastor. Perched high on the edge of the River Bijela's gorge, it was a modest white structure with a tall steeple. To reach it, we walked up through the village. It was the last hour before sunset—"the golden hour," as photographers call it, when the setting sun softens everything in its amber glow.

It was also an especially poignant hour that evening, as we were both aware of the night drawing nigh to Bosnia. But as we walked, there was still some sun, and children were still playing outside. Everyone smiled the moment they saw the brown-robed figure, and he smiled and waved back.

When we reached the church and mounted its steps, Father Svet paused and pointed to the rooftops below. "You see that house there, the one with the red door?" I nodded. "They're Croatian. And the house next to them with the bicycle in the yard?" I nodded again. "Serbs." He smiled. "And across the street? Muslims."

We stood in silence, looking down at the peaceful village in the lengthening shadows. Then he said, "The children play together in the street until their mothers call them in for supper. Then they come back out and play again. They don't know there's any difference between them."

He looked up at the mountains to the west, summits still burnished by the sun and wreathed below with smoky mist.

"When I think of the children," he said softly, "I think there is still hope for my country."

I left for Dubrovnik the following morning, driving fast down to the coast, then south along the Adriatic. It was another spectacular day, and to parallel the Neretva in broad daylight was an unforgettable experience.

The drive along the Adriatic Coast invited daydreaming of the days many years ago when old Alfas and Jaguars and Ferraris would dice through its curves. When the traffic thickened, I was not sorry, however, for each vista surpassed the one before, deserving full page after full page in the book of forever memories. The sea, which had earlier been a startling gray-blue, now reflected the copper sky, in which the sun was a vibrant crimson orb. Each inlet looked like a movie set, crammed with sailing vessels of every description—hand-carved figureheads, brightly painted fancywork, varnished decks and cabins, some so fanciful they might have been sets for an operetta.

When I reached Dubrovnik, I turned in the car and checked into the Belvedere, a mile south on the water. Normally staying there would have been impossible; at the height of the season, the newest of the five-star hotels would have been fully booked months in advance. But this evening my footfalls on the gray marble floor echoed in the deserted lobby. Only ten of the 440 beds were taken.

The PanAm office was closed; I would go there in the morning, and see what my options were. As the sun settled into the sea, I walked to the ancient walled city. On the way I noted that the cats of Dubrovnik were long in body like Egyptian cats, and mischievous and terribly thin. I befriended a coal-black one with yellow-green eyes who was willing to be stroked as long as I was willing to stroke him. When I stood up to resume my journey, he inquired if I might take him home with me. I explained that I lived a long way away over the water. He said that would be all right. I tried to explain that we already had two cats. He said he was used to company and would not ask them to leave. I shook my head and started to walk away. He followed a way, hoping I would change my mind, then gave up. I had heard that cats were precognitive—did he have an intimation of what was coming to his city?

Apparently the people of Dubrovnik did not. The commanders of Croatia's overmatched territorial defenders had been warning the city to dig in and set up defenses, but the city fathers had refused. The thousand-year-old "Jewel of the Adriatic" was a cultural treasure that belonged to the world, they told each other. Napoleon had respected this; even Hitler had left it alone. Surely the Serbs would not be the first in more than eight hundred years to desecrate this historic treasure.

That night Dubrovnik was filled with hundreds of young people from miles around who had come to walk the broad paving stones of the old city's main thoroughfare. They were laughing and happy, but there was a forced edge to their gaiety; it was as if by collective strength of will they sought to keep the war from coming there.

I was a curiosity that night—the only American in town. My fellow citizens had heeded the State Department's advisory, and the British had packed up as well. As a result the magazine kiosks didn't bother to stock any English language material. Having had no news since I arrived and with the war breaking out in Croatia, I would have settled for anything, even a week-old *Herald-Tribune*. After briefly joining the cadres of strolling young people and trying to enter into their unreality, I gave it up and went to bed.

The next morning the concierge had good news: PanAm

had relented and was sending one JFK-bound sweeper flight first to Sarajevo, then to Dubrovnik to round up stragglers. I qualified.

I had time for breakfast and went up to the dining room where I encountered the most magnificent breakfast buffet I had ever seen, suitable for a full complement of guests. The maître d' was impeccably attired in a morning coat. When I queried him why all this for ten guests, he explained that the owners were determined to carry on all the hotel's traditions as long as they were able. He spoke with admiration and affection, but it was evident that he regarded it as a *beau geste* which he would not have made had the decision been his.

I had the feeling that all of Dubrovnik was in denial. It reminded me of home, when a hurricane down in the Caribbean started to head north. Everyone on Cape Cod would watch the weather channel with morbid fascination as the whirling mass drew near. Always hoping that it would veer out to sea at the last minute, we would not board up the windows until just before all hell broke loose. I had been through such calms twice. It might be bright and sunny outside, but suddenly the birds fell silent, and the air became deathly still while overhead the clouds started moving in fast. One had about three hours then to board up the windows and lash down everything outside.

But Dubrovnik's garage had no hurricane boards, and the track of the approaching storm showed no signs of deviating.

An in-flight announcement in Italian and English requested that we return our seatbacks to their full, upright position; we were on our final descent into Rome. With difficulty I pulled loafers onto swollen feet, settled as comfortably as possible against my upright seatback, and resumed recollecting Bosnia. The next time I had returned was at Father Svet's request in December 1991.

In the wake of Slovenia and Croatia's declarations of independence, Bosnia-Hercegovina had shown signs of tilting in that direction as well. For sheer economic reasons, Serbia and Montenegro, who still called themselves Yugoslavia, could not afford to let Bosnia leave. Before Slovenia and Croatia broke away, those two republics had provided 55 percent of former Yugoslavia's gross national product (GNP). If now Bosnia left, that would be another 20 percent of the GNP. Meanwhile, they still had to support the huge JNA. Tito, deeply distrusting Stalin and fearful that he or his successors would one day turn on Yugoslavia as they had on other Eastern Bloc countries, had built the JNA into the fourth most powerful land army in Europe [Russia's being the first]. The deterrent had worked, but now Tito and Communism were gone, and the Red Army, like other post–Cold War armies, was undergoing a drastic, painful downsizing. The JNA, which had consumed an enormous amount of former Yugoslavia's GNP, had lost its *raison d'être*.

That is, until Slovenia and Croatia's departures had provided such an excellent reason for continuing to exist. The pretext of Serbian leader Slobodan Milosevic for sending the JNA into Croatia was to protect Serb enclaves there, though geopolitical analysts around the world labeled it an old-fashioned land-grab. "Greater Serbia" had always been a fond dream of Belgrade's; soon it could become a reality. The upper echelons of the JNA officer corps, being almost entirely Serbian, were ready to back Milosevic's play.

So when Bosnia's Muslims (44 percent of the populace) and Croats (18 percent) called for a national referendum on independence, Serbia and the Bosnian Serb leadership instructed Bosnia's Serbs (31 percent) to boycott the referendum. And just in case, in addition to the large regular army contingent already in Mostar, on September 20 they dispatched twenty thousand JNA reservists and Serb paramilitaries there "to ensure the safety of the civilian population."

That act prompted the U.S. ambassador in Belgrade to upgrade his advisory to a directive: All U.S. citizens still in Bosnia were to leave at once. In the absence of pilgrims and with the few phone lines into that country perpetually tied up, panic-fueled rumors began to circulate among Americans who had been to Bosnia. To give an accurate picture of the situation, Father Svet had urged me to come over.

I agreed and arranged to spend ten days there in mid-December 1991. Because of the United Nations sanctions against Serbia, the only way in was via JAT (Yugoslav Air Transport); I therefore had to kill an afternoon in Belgrade's airport before taking JAT's one daily flight to Sarajevo. The terminal was grim and grimy, with far fewer travelers than on my first visit and far more military police, now armed with submachine guns rather than side arms. Also, for foreigners there was now a "war tax" of seven dollars and a "security fee" of sixty dollars—my first indication of how desperate the Milosevic government was for hard currency.

Waging war was a hugely expensive undertaking, especially when one was mounting a full-scale offensive, as the Serbs were in Croatia. They had to meet army payrolls, and with no foreign countries willing to extend them a loan, Belgrade had no choice but to start printing money. For years before the war, the exchange rate had held steadily at seven dinars to the dollar. When I was there in July, the rate had doubled. Now, according to the exchange booth in the terminal, it was triple. But a few feet away in the coffee shop, a dollar was worth sixty dinars.

Arriving at Sarajevo after ten, I found the terminal totally deserted, save for a dozen cab drivers hoping for a fare. We had been told ground transportation would be waiting for those heading south to Mostar, but there was none. I smiled. In Bosnia, even before the war, travel arrangements were never as nailed-down as you were used to at home. The trick was to keep your sense of humor and improvise. Three other Americans were heading south; we decided to carpool, and I hired one of the drivers.

Sarajevo had just had a major winter storm, and the roads were treacherous—three inches of snow on top of an inch of ice. The beautiful road down to Mostar had fallen into disrepair, not because of shelling, but because there were no funds for maintenance. I asked our driver, a young Muslim, why he was out on a night like this. Simple, he said. He had five mouths to feed: he and his wife had two children and a dog named Brik. Also, because of the sanctions, the only heating oil to be had was on the black market and was extremely expensive.

We reached the outskirts of Mostar a little after 3:00 A.M., where we picked up an escort. We had just passed a parked car, when it flicked on its lights and started following us. Police, I thought, except that we had not been speeding. At the next streetlight they pulled alongside of us. They weren't police; they were swarthy, scruffy-looking men in their thirties—wearing mustaches, unshaven, and grinning.

"Do not look at them!" the driver hissed, keeping his own eyes straight ahead as the light changed. He turned left; so did the other car. He turned left again; the other car did the same. I remembered hearing somewhere that the civilian irregulars loosely affiliated with the paramilitaries around Mostar were former convicts. They had been released from prison and given guns, and their leader was wanted in Australia on six counts of murder. Now I was afraid. Cold-sweat afraid.

We arrived at the Hotel Ruja, where two white military vehicles were parked in front with a circle of blue stars on their doors. "E.C.," our driver exclaimed with relief; they belonged to the European Community monitoring team assigned to Mostar. Our escort disappeared. But the Ruja had no oil and sent us to the Dom Pensione, where we now proceeded, without escort.

At the curb in front of the Dom's front door, there was a blackened crater. Our driver said it had been on the news: a police cruiser had been blown up there the night before. We hurried inside.

In the towns and villages of eastern Croatia, the police were the first targets. Civilian irregulars (such as the men who had shadowed us?) would slip into town and fire on the police, who would defend themselves. The JNA would then come in with their tanks "to restore order"—and never leave. And the irregulars would move on to the next town.

In the morning I connected with Father Svet, who was chaplain now at Bijelo Polje on the outskirts of Mostar, the mother house of the Franciscan Sisters in Hercegovina. He took me on a walking tour of Mostar. The sun was out, and no snow was here. The day was bright and crisp, and tiny bits of mica in the sidewalk sparkled like a field of diamonds. Mostar was incredibly charming. There were outdoor cafés, but they were all closed now, and the shade trees that lined the streets were bare. But if the city was this beautiful in winter, what must it be like in summer?

It was not hard to imagine: These magnificent old trees would make a cool, inviting canopy of shade on the hottest of days, like the *Bois de Boulogne* in Paris. They would encourage strollers as Paris did, and the white café tables would be filled with people talking, drinking coffee, or just taking the sun. Paris was the best city for drifting on a summer day, because of the surprises waiting around so many corners. Mostar was like Paris in miniature.

Another young couple passed us, arm in arm; apparently Mostar, too, was for lovers.

But now the music on the soundtrack in my mind shifted to a minor key. Others were out walking this morning—men in brown uniforms. They didn't look like soldiers; they had long hair and stubbled chins, and they slouched along in twos and threes. They looked bored, and some obviously had been drinking that morning. I asked Father Svet if they were JNA, and he shook his head. They were reservists or paramilitaries.

One thing they all had in common, I noted: long bayonets affixed to their belts. "They are looking for trouble," Father Svet explained, "hoping to create an incident that will give the JNA the excuse to impose martial law." He shook his head. "But the people of Mostar know this and refuse to be provoked."

A truckload full of soldiers rumbled by, and I revised my earlier comparison: Mostar *was* like Paris—in June 1940.

That afternoon we hiked up a rocky hill together, and at the top I asked him if he thought the war would come to Bosnia. It seemed to me that the present situation was tense but holding, though the feeling was of a forest that had not had any rain for weeks; the slightest spark could set it ablaze.

He thought for a moment. "There is something I am even afraid to say." He paused. "I don't know what will be the outcome of the next days, the next months. . . . One would like to shorten that journey." He sighed, then concluded,

"Who knows, we may be called to go the whole length of it."

We picked our way down in silence. Abruptly he stopped and looked at me. "If you were me, and the war came right here, would you stay? Or would you leave?"

I laughed, hoping to lighten the mood. "Happily that won't be your decision; your provincial will decide for you."

But he did not smile. He was the most serious I had ever seen him.

"There is a tradition among us Franciscans," he said. "When it comes to that, each man must make his own decision."

I was deeply sad. "Then you will stay. There will be people who will need you, and you will not leave them."

"Absolutely!" he exclaimed with a grin and headed down the path.

———————————

Outside the airplane's window, buildings were flashing past. The wheels chirped, and the pilot reversed engines. We were in Rome.

FOUR

INCIDENT AT KONJIC

The blow at the base of the windshield had left circular concussion fractures like ripples in a pond, with one longer crack beginning to angle up toward the center of the driver's vision. It was not too bad now, but it was not going to improve with age. I did not mind the cracks until the highbeams of an oncoming car hit them.

We were driving south along the Adriatic, before turning inland. If you were a civilian flying from the United States to Bosnia in the summer of 1996, you could not get here from there. The airports at Sarajevo and Mostar were closed to commercial traffic. The two routes into Bosnia went through Croatia: from Frankfurt to Zagreb and drive south, or from Rome to Split and drive north. We had chosen the latter.

Traveling with me on this trip was Luke Norman, a producer for Paraclete Video Productions who was doing a "reckie"[5] to see if there might be a documentary in postwar Bosnia. Luke was a Texan from our community, about twenty years younger than I. We were both tall, but he was thin, and I wasn't. He was a meticulous planner, and I wasn't. And he always got his work done on time, and I didn't. He

---

[5] British commando lingo for a reconnaissance mission. The BBC had picked it up from them, and PVP had picked it up from a BBC friend.

was also preternaturally calm in tense situations, while my own feelings were usually right on the surface; I could become calm, but it took a while. (It turned out that inwardly he was reacting the same way I was, only I did not find that out until Sarajevo.)

We left the coast at Makarska and headed into the mountains and heavy fog. I turned the wheel over to Luke, who had slept on the flight over; by my reckoning, it had been forty hours since I had slept. But there was no dozing now. With no guardrail, the sudden hairpin turns kept us both alert. Occasionally an enormous truck would loom out of the darkness, forcing us to the edge of the road, or a big Mercedes would overtake us. In America such cars were not rare, but over here they were comparatively scarce; anyone driving one was very important. Ordinary people deferred to them, getting out of their way quickly; a Mercedes never had to use its horn.

No one deferred to the car we were driving: an old Ford Escort, loaned to us by Jeff Reed. I had met Jeff through Father Svet. When the war broke out in Croatia, he had been one of the first to be galvanized into action on behalf of the refugees. By the end of 1991, a hundred thousand people had been driven out of their homes—and the war had not yet spilled over into Bosnia. A business executive in Dallas, Jeff had been instrumental in organizing truck convoys of badly needed food and supplies from the United Kingdom to Croatia. In his church, St. David's Episcopal, he set up a relief organization. With frequent trips to Bosnia taking up more and more of his time, he finally made relief his vocation instead of avocation. His organization now had an office in Split, and Jeff had given them the use of the car he had shipped from home when he was not using it himself.

As the war had gathered momentum, Jeff and I had

become friends. For the first year of the war, the media and the State Department had seemed strangely disinterested in the events in Bosnia. So those of us with friends over here had set up a fax network to relay reliable news to those who cared. The faxes were immediately refaxed and reprinted in newsletters and magazines; in this way a great many people could be brought up to date quickly. Jeff was a hub on that network.

When it came time to arrange a vehicle for this trip, I had found renting a car impossible. So many cars had been "commandeered" at gunpoint that the insurance was astronomical, especially if you were planning to cross borders as we were. The only way to acquire a car was to hire a driver/interpreter, whose meals and accommodations would be our responsibility. That was fine if you were the BBC, but this trip was self-financed, and the expense was prohibitive. Besides, I had a hunch we could get along without an interpreter. Whenever I had been to Bosnia (or anywhere else in Europe), I had always found someone who could speak some English. Most Bosnian children were learning it as a second language.

As I was lamenting the car situation on the phone to Jeff one day, he had said, "Why don't you use my car? You can pick it up at the Split office when you land. I'll call and set it up. Watch out for the potholes up north," he advised, "and be careful where you park. Cars are still disappearing up there, especially if they have Croatian plates. But," he added in his slow Texan drawl, "if anything does happen to the car, don't worry about it. That's why it's a small one, not a big one."[6]

As our headlights did their best to penetrate the fog, we lapsed into silence. Looking at the pattern of the cracks in

---

[6] Anyone looking for a reliable Bosnian relief agency cannot do better than St. David's Relief Foundation, 5458 O'Banion Road, Garland, TX 75043.

the windshield, I recalled Jeff's telling me of the incident when it had happened. A Croatian refugee who had been born and lived all his life in Konjic (the town on the Neretva, in whose monastery I had worked with Father Svet) had passed away. His dying wish had been to be buried in the family plot in the town's old cemetery. For centuries Konjic had had a small but thriving Croatian community which in 1991 numbered some thirteen thousand. In the latter stages of the war, when the Muslims and Croats realized that even together they were not strong enough to repel the Serbs, they turned on each other. In Konjic the Muslims did to the Croats what further south the Croats were doing to the Muslims, and what the Serbs had done to both of them everywhere they could: they ethnically cleansed the minority from their midst. Fewer than a thousand Croats remained in Konjic, most of them too old to move.

The son of the deceased man, a Franciscan priest stationed in Mostar, decided to respect his father's wish. Accompanied by his priest friends (one of whom was Father Svet) and Jeff in this car, he made the hour-and-a-half drive north to bury his father. Had they been the only ones to come, the burial might have passed without incident. But the deceased had many friends who like himself were now refugees down on the coast. They, too, wanted to come back to bury their friend. So they hired a bus and joined the cortege.

As they drove through town, people shouted at them, telling them that they had better turn around while they still could. The procession went on to the cemetery, parked, and accompanied the casket to the graveside. There the son conducted a burial service for his father. One old woman in the group, frightened by the threats they had received, whispered to the priest to hurry, but the service proceeded with stately solemnity.

When they had lowered the casket into the grave and said their last prayer, the burial party walked back to their cars. Every windshield and every rearview mirror of every car with Mostar plates had been smashed. And the bus was nowhere to be seen. The message was clear: Do not think of returning, not even to bury your dead.

I was stunned. It was one thing to read about such things in the newspaper; it was quite another to hear about it from a friend who had been there.

When I called Father Svet to tell him when we were coming, I asked him about it. With a sad voice he confirmed the details. As he did, I thought back to the evening we had walked up to his little church at sundown. Serbs and Muslims had waved to us. So had Croats. They were just Bosnians then, their children playing together in the street.

Father Svet then told me of another event that had happened that weekend about four miles away in the little village of Spiljani. It, too, involved a burial at a cemetery. Another family, also returning to bury an older member, did so on Saturday afternoon. The next morning they went back to put fresh flowers on the grave. During the night someone, knowing that they would return, had planted a mine next to the grave. A ten-year-old girl had stepped on it and had her leg blown off.

I was sickened at the act and at the mind that could conceive of such a thing. My second reaction was fury. But Father Svet had witnessed so many atrocities, counseled so many victims, he was just deeply sad.

Thinking about it in the car, I became furious all over again. If they ever caught someone like that, and I were the judge, I would have no trouble thinking of a punishment to fit the crime. I began to run down some suitable options. . . .

And then stopped, struck by the realization that this

was exactly the line of thinking that kept the cycle of hatred alive in Bosnia, or northern Ireland, or wherever. It could live for twenty, forty, a hundred years, because each generation nurtured it and passed it on to the next. "Listen, lad, you want to know why we don't want you playing with their children? Let me tell you what three of them did to your grandmother. . . ."

Despite the youth of his listener, the narrator would spare no details, no matter how sordid. He *wanted* the scene implanted in the boy's mind for the rest of his life. The greater the shock, the greater the subsequent fury.

"The sons of those who did it are still alive. Now come here; I want to show you something. You see this? It belonged to your grandfather. I put it away until you were old enough. This is a Kalashnikov, Russian-made; they call it an AK-47. Originally it was your grandfather's, and he killed eight of them with it. You're not old enough for it yet, but you will be one day, and then we'll see if you can use it as well as he did."

I suddenly thought, *what if it had been* my *grandmother?* What if it had been my wife, and someone had handed me that gleaming, oiled weapon of swift revenge? What if I knew where the perpetrators lived, and my brother-in-law were ready to come with me?

Vengeance is mine, saith the Lord.

Would I have listened? I didn't know. But I did know that the new Bosnia was going to show me things I didn't want to see about what humankind could do; and about myself.

"Checkpoint," Luke announced, slowing the car. Up ahead on the left, a raised barrier was silhouetted by a floodlight. Behind it in the fog, two uniformed men were caught in the light from the open doorway of the guard-house. One lowered the barrier and signaled for us to stop.

The only color in that black-and-white tableau was the orange glow of a cigarette, briefly intensifying as the other man inhaled.

"Must be the border," I said, stating the obvious. "They didn't stop me last time."

"Maybe you were on the right road," Luke observed. "When we took that turn half an hour ago, neither of us felt good about it."

I nodded. "This is definitely the road less traveled."

The border guard at the barrier now approached the car. Luke handed him our passports which he took inside the guardhouse. We waited. The other guard lit another cigarette. I would have liked a cigarette myself—and I hadn't smoked in thirty years. I drummed my fingers on the dashboard. "Wonder what's taking him so long," I murmured. Luke, preternaturally calm, just shrugged.

Finally the guard with our passports emerged, frowning, and went over to the other, who was senior. They looked at our passports and looked at us.

"What *is* the matter?" I whispered, unnerved.

Luke shrugged again. "Maybe we're the only car they've had in an hour."

"Maybe we're the only Americans they've had all night."

"Just keep smiling," he said, doing just that.

They came over. The senior guard asked Luke something in Bosnian. "Sorry, only English," Luke replied. The guard pointed at us and made a gesture of inquiry.

"American journalists," Luke explained.

It was a term recognizable in any language, and they nodded and smiled. The guard with the passports handed them back.

"Medjugorje?" asked Luke, pointing ahead.

The guard shook his head. "Ljubuski."

"Ljubuski is good," I said to Luke. "It's not far from the village." And bed, I almost added; Medjugorje was only half an hour away.

The other guard raised the barrier, and in a moment we were in Bosnia.

FIVE

ORDINARY PEOPLE

Medjugorje — An old woman in black emerged from the tall doors into the bright sun. At noon the heat and humidity were oppressive, the broad plaza in front of the church was deserted. Even so, it was surprising to see it so empty; for the first time in five years Medjugorje was full of pilgrims. Everyone was out of the sun, except this old woman.

Leaning heavily on her cane, she shuffled to the first step and stopped. From her left hand hung two bulky bags; she adjusted them and waited, perhaps gathering strength for the descent or hoping someone might come and help. Someone did. Appearing from the church behind her, a middle-aged woman gently slipped an arm under hers and half-lifted, helping her down step by step until she was on level ground.

The old woman gave a nod of thanks and set off slowly across the plaza, a solitary black figure moving over a sea of bright stone. Her destination: the white marble statue of the *Gospa* at the left front of the plaza. Around the statue was a circle of benches, empty now because of the heat. Was she aware of it through the black dress, black sweater, black stockings, and babushka? Or was the heat minor, compared to other pain?

Reaching one of the benches, she carefully laid down the packages and placed the cane where it could be easily retrieved. She sat directly in front of the statue and gazed up at its face. For a long time she didn't move.

For a long time I watched her. She represented a part of Bosnia that had always been there.

Down the street leading to the church, people were strolling or browsing in the shops or meeting friends for lunch in one of the many restaurants. I remembered what it had been like when I had been here in December 1991. It was a ghost town. The restaurants had been shuttered, and if any of the little shops and stalls selling rosaries, crucifixes, and plaster statuettes was open, it was only because the proprietor didn't have anything else to do. The only movement on the street were bits of dry shrub blown by the wind—like sagebrush, I had thought gloomily.

That afternoon had been as cold as today was hot, and I had asked my guide, Slavica (who was also our guide on this visit), where we could get some hot coffee. American coffee. She took me across the street to the one restaurant still open: the old Dubrovnik Café. A favorite meeting place, it had enough local clientele to keep going. We went downstairs into the Bavarian-style rathskeller. At two tables in the back were about two dozen young men, drinking beer and singing. Only these songs weren't the kind that guys sang around a barroom piano; the sound in them was of pride and fire and steel.

They were a group of volunteers, Slavica had explained, on their way to join the Territorial Defense Force. And the songs were battle songs, some two centuries old. The one they were singing now called on an ancient duke who had been a hero of Croatia to rise up and help them in their time of need.

Listening to them, I got goosebumps; they reminded me of German war movies. And they were compelling. They drew one into their spirit. I could imagine myself as one of these *camaraden*, ready to shoulder my rifle and march off with them.

The song ended, but the words seemed to linger in the old rafters. I took a sip of coffee, and gradually the spell died away.

They were so eager to get into the fighting. Well, they would not have long to wait; earlier in the day I had spotted a new outpost established by Serb paramilitaries just outside Milakovici, barely six miles away. They had been on field maneuvers, and the sun had glinted on their brown helmets as they scurried through the underbrush. They looked like brown beetles.

A waitress brought the young warriors another round of beer, and they started to sing again. Only now the movie in my mind was French, not German, and it was about the First World War, not the Second. I had seen this movie before, and this was only the first reel. In the second reel they go through their first mind-numbing artillery barrage, which hurls their world skyward, deafening them, frightening them as nothing ever has before. In a matter of days they become young-old men with dull eyes and dead expressions. In the last reel they are ordered to leave the safety of their position and charge an enemy machine-gun nest. They do. Bravery counts for nothing. Youth, noble ideas, hopes, love—the machine gun doesn't care, as it calmly, efficiently mows them all down. In the final scene all is quiet as young wives and old women in black pick through the broken trees and crumbled buildings, turning over bodies casually flung aside, looking for the faces they are afraid to find.

Only this was no movie.

After that trip, I had come back in November of 1992. The war in Bosnia had been going on for nine months, and the front had stabilized. There was still shooting in Mostar, but in this area and all the way to Makarska, the Territorial Defense Force was firmly in control. Word began to filter out that if pilgrims stuck to the back roads, it was reasonably safe for them to return. A few began to, and I among them.

From the village, Mostar was thirteen crow-miles away, but at twilight, if the air was still, you could hear the *crump, crump* of shells exploding there. And in the hills nearby you could hear the occasional rip of a submachine gun or the burst of small-arms fire. Target practice was the official explanation, though I was inclined to believe the private, wry assessment of a local: some of the boys had gotten into the plum brandy and developed an itch on their trigger fingers.

While it was unsafe to run the gauntlet of Serb gunners holding the mountains around Mostar (though Father Svet did it regularly), here in the village there was an almost supernatural tranquillity.

Now, five years later, peace had indeed returned. During the war, Citluk, three miles away to the north, had been shelled and bombed from the air, Ljubuski to the east had been hit, and to the south, Capljina had been badly hammered. But Medjugorje had come through the war unscathed—about the only war-zone village in Bosnia that had. To be sure, local families had lost loved ones in the fighting; everyone had. But in the village of Medjugorje total casualties had been one cow and one dog.

Once again a building boom was on with a host of new souvenir shops lining the main street where eight years before, gypsies had sold rosaries from the trunks of their old Mercedes. The street itself had been widened to accommodate tour buses, which now clogged it. Some pilgrims who had come in the early years lamented the creeping commercialization and the fact that some of the villagers now had nice cars and color television sets. (They should try the Holy Land; the commercialization of Medjugorje, compared with that of Jerusalem, is like comparing a Boy Scout Jamboree with World War II.)

But the spirit emanating from the village had not changed; it still had that night-before-Christmas effect on people. And it was self-reinforcing: liking the way they felt, the pilgrims tried even harder to be caring and sensitive. It was like being in Shangri-la, that mythical place where everyone behaved the way they wished everyone else would. It was what believers called *agape* love. And it was fun.

It also seemed totally out of character with the rest of Bosnia, until it occurred to me that Bosnia was like the human soul. In a soul are pools of light, so luminous they produce a glow on the night horizon. But there are also dismal swamps, from which a darkness exudes that threatens to seep into all the soul's corners. The eternal question is: which will prevail?

Whether one accepted the veracity of apparitions or not, no one could deny that Medjugorje was encouraging the light to shine in millions of souls, including many who had only read or heard about it. As for those who had actually come, I did not know of one whose heart was not touched. Many had had their lives changed. Like David du Plessis, I had come as a fruit inspector, and as far as I could tell, the fruit from this tree was only good.

Then how could the war have come here, with Medjugorje happening in Bosnia's backyard, as it were? How could so many Bosnians, including Catholic Croats, have behaved so reprehensibly toward one another?

Once during the war, I asked that question of Sister Janja, an old friend who had been the superior of the convent in Mostar throughout the bombardment. The phone connection was terrible, but her answer was clear: "Medjugorje is a challenge. If it is true, then people must change. They must convert; they have no choice. God must become the most important thing in their lives."

I agreed, but what was she getting at?

"Think how threatening conversion is. If they have power, they may have to give it up. If they have money, they may have to give it away. If they are carrying hate, they *will* have to let it go. Whatever happens, their entire lives will be turned upside down and will never be the same." She paused. "So, anyone who does not want to change must ignore Medjugorje—even Croats who think they are religious."

I remembered the young men in the rathskeller, looking forward to going to war. Medjugorje itself could not stop the war. But it *had* stopped the war in millions of hearts. And it *was* part of the whole picture of Bosnia—it was the part that provided the balance. By inspiring ordinary people, it made them somehow more than ordinary.

———————————

The clocks on the twin spires of St. James Church both said it was half past twelve. The plaza was empty; except for the old woman in black and an older American couple who sat in the shade of the nearest cedars, about thirty paces from the statue. They, too, were watching it, and had been for more than an hour. The man wore khakis and a red polo shirt and sensible running shoes; the woman had hinged sunshades over her eyeglasses and a blue flight bag with "206 Tours" on it.

On an impulse, I went over and sat down next to them. Their name tags said they were Don and Diane.[7] What were they doing out in the noonday sun? Waiting for a Croatian orphan named Marija, a thirteen-year-old whom they had foster-adopted but had never met. They were going to take her home with them to America.

Don had served in submarines during the war, after which he had become an insurance executive, retiring in 1989. Coming to Medjugorje had been Diane's idea, and he, though not particularly interested, had agreed to go with her. They were to come in November of 1991, and while the war had not yet come to Bosnia, it was raging in Croatia. At the last minute a friend of Diane's had a frightening premonition that something terrible was going to happen to them if they went. Diane backed out. Don went on alone.

He came home spiritually deepened, as he put it, but he had no idea how much, until he came back the following year with his wife. She loved Medjugorje, but he was disappointed; it wasn't like before. In the Mass, the priests' robes were just white—not gleaming like freshly fallen snow. And their vestments were just green—not a fiery emerald green that seemed iridescent. And the choir was just village kids singing—not with voices so clear it seemed as if angels had come down to join them. That was when he realized the depth of what had happened to him on his first trip.

Something terrible happened after they returned home. A grandchild, Lisa, and two other two-year-old girls were playing on a slide at a day-care center. The supervisor had gone inside to get a cup of coffee, and while she was gone, Lisa had slipped, and the cord of her windbreaker had

---

[7] Here and elsewhere, to preserve privacy, some names, places, and details have been changed.

caught, hanging her by the neck. One of her playmates ran inside to try to get a grown-up to come help, but by the time someone came, Lisa had been unable to breathe for several minutes.

They had airlifted her by helicopter to the hospital, but the doctors did not hold out much hope; she had been too long without oxygen. Her brain showed no response to stimulation, and when she opened her eyes in intensive care, the left pupil was down in the left-hand corner of the eye socket, and the right pupil was down in the right. At best, it was feared she would be a vegetable as long as she lived.

Had I not asked them for their story, at this point I would have changed the subject or left. A powerful imagination could be a mixed blessing. I had a two-year-old granddaughter, Sharon, and in my mind I could not help seeing her playing, slipping, hanging, and then—not responding. It was chilling.

Emotions flooded through Don—anguish, frustration, despair—and when the tempest subsided, he knew what he must do. In Medjugorje he and Diane had come to believe in the power of prayer. So they started praying, and they called praying friends and asked them to pray. They even called a couple in Australia whom they had met on their pilgrimage. Prayer was going up around the world.

Diane prayed one prayer over and over, until it became a part of her: "God, please hold her in your arms and heal her."

After two weeks the doctors sent Lisa home; there was nothing more they could do for her. She could not hear or communicate, had no use of her arms or legs, and was blind. But she could feel pain; when she awoke, her back would be arched, until her medication took effect. Don and Diane spent as much time as they could with her. They bought a wagon with wooden sides and pulled her everywhere, talking to her, loving her. It took two of them; one to pull, the other to keep the sun out of her eyes, because Lisa couldn't close them or turn her head.

A month after the accident, they went back to Medjugorje, Diane to pray her prayer, Don to fulfill a vow he had made while Lisa was in the hospital. On the first day he climbed both Podbrdo and Mount Krizevac. It took him most of the day. He repeated it the next day and every day thereafter, until they went home.

When they got home, there was an amazing improvement in Lisa: she was responding to her environment, and her faculties were beginning to come back. Don and Diane redoubled their prayers and soon came back to Medjugorje, this time to give thanks. And to give something back.

At the time of the first apparition in June 1981, the pastor of St. James Church was Father Jozo Zovko. When Communist officials and police had come hunting the six young children who claimed to be seeing the *Gospa* every afternoon, he had protected them. Rather than condemn the apparitions as a hoax, he had gone to prison for a year and a half. Now he had a powerful ministry of his own, and at the time the war broke out, he had been guardian of the monastery at Siroki Brijeg, an hour away. To Father Jozo, the most tragic victims of the war were the children who had lost one or both parents. He set up the Save-the-Children program for foster parents to adopt these orphans. Foster parents would agree to send $50 a month to help with their support. More important, they would send love, writing personal letters to let the children know that someone cared for them.

Don and Diane adopted two of these orphans. They never met them, but the children sent pictures of themselves and letters. Then Don and Diane came back to Medjugorje and adopted four more.

Their second, Marija, was now thirteen and living with an aunt in Tihaljina. She was studying English in school and began writing Don and Diane in English. Her letters were full of what she was doing and who her friends were, and in their replies, they would ask how she was doing in school and what she hoped to do. Then a few months ago, they asked something else: How would she like to come to America for the summer? Through her aunt and the Save-the-Children program, they arranged for a two-month visit.

They had arranged to meet Marija and her aunt for the first time today or tomorrow after the English Mass at the statue of the *Gospa*. It would probably be tomorrow. They had been waiting for almost two hours, and whenever a young girl of about the right age stopped there, Don would go up with a piece of paper on which was written: "Marija?" He'd had no luck so far, but he was not discouraged.

"You know," he said, "no matter how this turns out, this child and the others will be as close to us as one of our grandchildren."

And how was Lisa now?

Her vision was fine now. She still had a problem with balance; she fell down easily. And there was still a bit of a problem with her small-motor muscles. But there was no problem with her mouth motor; she talked all the time. And her mind was perfect; she would be starting kindergarten in the fall.

Gazing up at Mount Krizevac, Diane remembered something that Lisa had said about a year after the accident. She had been sitting on the floor playing, when for no reason she looked up at Diane and said, "When you die, you go to

Heaven. I died when I was a baby and went to Heaven, and God held me in His arms."

I left them there and walked across the plaza and up the steps that the old woman had come down two hours before. One of the benches on the side terrace extended into a shady corner near the end of the row of confessionals. No one was around. I settled there and gazed up at Mount Krizevac. In the haze of the early afternoon, the large concrete cross on top seemed almost white.

I was remembering something that had happened on my first visit here. In the old village cemetery far back from the church, shaded by a stand of cedars, I had lain on my back on the carpet of pine needles, looking at the sky. I had asked God what He wanted of me, and the thought had come: *You already know. Surrender.*

I promised that I would. Soon.

For the next seven years I had yielded to Him and let Him cross my will countless ways. I had completed four books and accumulated numerous accolades. But I had not surrendered. Not unconditionally. Not to the point where I gave up reserving the right to make the final decision.

Then came St. Patrick's Day a year ago. At the time I was swimming every day and thought I was in the best shape of my life. But one night there was blood in my urine. When I called our doctor, Bill Velie, I told him I was sure I'd just popped a minor blood vessel swimming a mile time-trial. He agreed but still insisted I get abdominal x-rays. So I went to Cape Cod Hospital on March 17.

If the radiology nurse ever comes back in smiling and says, "The doctor would just like to get another angle," be concerned. If she then comes back and says, "Now he would like to get some ultrasound pictures," be very concerned.

Next, she told me to call my doctor. "Look," Bill said, when I got him on the phone, "they've found something. I want you to talk to the urologist on duty there."

I caught him when he came out of the operating room while they were anesthetizing his patient. He said, "I don't have enough time to break this to you gently, so I am just going to show it to you." He put my x-ray up on the wall light-table. "This is a normal kidney," he tapped the left one on the x-ray, "and this," he tapped a dense protrusion on the right one which made it a third larger than the other, "is cancer."

I stared at him, open-mouthed. My denial phase lasted all of three seconds.

Seeing my expression, he smiled. "Look, you've still got the other one." The smile faded. "We're going to need a bone scan and a CAT scan to see if it's spread." He wrote down his office address. "See my secretary; she'll set up the appointments." And with that his pager went off, and he had to go back into the operating room.

I drove home from the hospital, numb. Six years before, my father had died of stomach cancer. The first indication that there was anything wrong was blood in his urine. Eight months later he was gone. Eight months. In my mind I started getting my affairs in order, trying to think of all the things I needed to tell Barbara. Then I thought about the funeral.

In the past, I had said that I did not want one of those Victorious-Christian funerals, where everyone was so glad the deceased had gone home to be with Jesus. I wanted people *miserable* that I was gone, and had arranged the saddest funeral I could think of. The first hymn would be "Abide with Me" and the capper would be "Nearer My God to

Thee"—all eight verses. No one could sing all eight verses of that hymn without tearing up. Then I had picked three people to speak, each of whom I knew could not get halfway through before they broke down. I wanted all handkerchiefs out, the entire congregation awash with grief.

But now that it was actually going to happen, I felt differently. Russian anthems would be good—the ones that lifted you up into the presence of God and held you there.

When I got home, Barbara and Bill Velie were waiting in the kitchen. Taking one look at my face, Bill said, "Why don't we take one step back from the graveside. You'll still have the other kidney, and they're optimistic that the cancer hasn't escaped."

As it turned out, it hadn't. Though it had come within one millimeter of breaking out. If I had not swum that mile. . . .

"You know," said the admitting nurse when I went in for the operation, "it's really a miracle they caught this. We call kidney and bladder cancer the hidden killers. By the time you realize there's something wrong, it's too late." I knew. That was how a good friend and great writer, Jamie Buckingham, had died three years before.

The operation lasted five hours. The surgeon was confident they had gotten it all. In the recovery room they told me to push the button on the end of the cord whenever I felt pain. They had found that the patient actually administered less morphine than would a nurse on a set schedule. Three hours later they took me to my room, where they hooked up lots of wires to monitors, inserted a catheter, and ran an IV tube into my arm and an oxygen tube into my nostrils. On my legs they put compression stockings which would squeeze them once a minute, to prevent blood clots from forming.

Everything was on automatic pilot, and I assumed that

included the pain medication which I imagined was coming in regulated doses down the IV with whatever else was dripping into me. (Somewhere I had lost the cord with the button on the end.)

After about an hour I was beginning to feel serious pain and rang for the nurse. "Can you increase the morphine? I am really hurting."

"I'm sorry, sir, but the dosage is preset; you can get only so much an hour."

Two hours later, it was three in the morning and the pain was so bad I could not move. I was curled up in a ball, whispering the word "Jesus" over and over. I rang for the nurse and told her the pain was now unbelievable. She repeated what she had told me before, a little impatient and thinking I was exaggerating.

At 7:30 the day nurse came on and found me in the same position. I had not moved in four hours.

"We are going to have to get you to stand up, sir."

"Stand up? I can't even move my arm."

"I'm sorry, but we're going to have to help you. It's the procedure." She and her assistant got on either side of me and started to raise me up.

I screamed. The monitor showed my pulse surging wildly. I could breathe only in little gasps; my left lung had partially collapsed. Though they didn't say so, they thought I was having a heart attack, and so did I. They did sound a code blue, and suddenly all the interns in their green smocks came rushing in, with a portable x-ray and the paddles, everything.

I was scared already, but when none of these experts could figure out what was wrong with me, I became more scared than I had ever been in my life. If all the king's horses, and all the king's men. . . .

Finally, the oldest of the young doctors turned to me:

"You have been administering your painkiller, haven't you?"

"What do you mean? I thought it was going in the IV."

His eyes widened. "You mean—you have not had any painkiller in," he looked at the chart, "*nine hours?*"

We looked at each other speechless. Then he relaxed. "All right," he told the others, "now we know what the problem is." The rest of them relaxed. He put an arm on my shoulder. "I wish we could do something for you right away, but we can't. We're going to have to bring you up to tolerance gradually." He looked at his watch. "By noon you should be caught up."

He was right. By noon I was feeling no pain. In fact, I was on some kind of expanded-clarity high. It wasn't the drugs; it was the fact that I was alive, when I had thought I was going to die. I felt as I had right after the chute popped, the first (and last) time I had jumped out of an airplane. As the condemned man awaiting the hangman said, it wonderfully concentrated the mind. I understood everything.

Just then the phone range. It was an old friend whose spiritual wisdom I had relied on for many years. She was caring and supportive, and when she realized I was lucid and wanted to talk, she got down to brass tacks. She said that God had given me an extension of my life for a reason. Did I know what it was? Surrender, I replied. Living for Him totally, instead of striking percentage bargains. And I was ready: I felt like Scrooge, when he threw open the window and found he hadn't missed Christmas after all. She helped me sort out some relationships which had long been troubling me and made some suggestions of how I could start becoming the person I wanted to be. Then she showed me some things about myself which I had never seen before (or been able to see or been ready to see).

We talked for an hour and a half. It was the most

bedrock honest I had ever been with another human being. At the end, I said, "I am so grateful to have seen what you have shown me, that I would go through last night again if that was the price I had to pay for this level of understanding." And I meant it.

Now, looking up at that distant cross, I realized that while my life had changed since then, it had not changed as much as it should have. I was trying, but finding that surrender was a day-by-day, layer-by-layer process. And every time I thought that maybe I was getting somewhere, something would come up that would show me how far I still had to go.

That evening, I saw Don and Diane again. All that day Don stayed in the vicinity of the church. The logical thing would have been to come back the next day after the English Mass, since that had been their arrangement, but he could not bring himself to leave.

He didn't mind; the church was the center of activity in Medjugorje. It was like a magnet: pilgrims kept circling back to it. A long time ago when I was studying the French, I had been told of a saying about the Champs Élysées in Paris: If you sat at one of those outdoor cafés long enough, everyone you knew would pass by. The same might be said of the outside benches at St. James.

Don sat there as the late afternoon shadows lengthened, and the Croatian Mass began. Every so often, he would get up and have a look around. He did not see any likely candidates, but he still had a sense of peace. When Mass was over, it was dark, save for a few outdoor lights, and his wife joined the line at the English-language confessional.

Don was sitting on the bench, watching Mount Krizevac become a silhouette, when a young girl came up to him and said, "Excuse me, do you speak English?" She was blond and shy. Reading his name tag, she smiled. "I'm Marija."

SIX

LOST SHEPHERD

Siroki Brijeg — Bosnia was a beautiful country. It had been before the war, and it still was. The war had deeply scarred the people and their cities and villages. But it had not changed the land. When the weather was good, it was still a delight to drive anywhere in Bosnia (well, almost anywhere). On the Saturday that Luke and I drove over to Siroki Brijeg to see Father Svet, the weather was perfect. Through dusty hamlets, over winding mountain roads, past rich, green fields—everywhere the countryside was in full bloom. The monastery, church, library, and seminary were high on a hill overlooking a valley town that seemed to be taking a Saturday afternoon nap. What little traffic passed by down there seemed to be moving in slow motion.

On that particular Saturday all the Franciscan sisters in Hercegovina, more than 150 of them, were at the monastery for their annual "day of recollection." Father Svet had his hands full, leading a day-long retreat for them. He popped out to greet us, then left us on our own till the retreat ended. That was fine with us; we wandered around the large tree-shaded courtyard in front of the church, absorbing the peace and beauty of that place. The sunlight fell in shifting patterns through the trees, while the twin stone towers of the church, in full sunlight, stood out in stark relief against the cerulean sky.

From the open door of the church came the sound of singing. I slipped inside and stood in the shadows at the back of the nave. A choir of twenty or so sisters was singing an old anthem, their voices so in unison that they sounded like one person.

Eventually Father Svet joined us. He introduced us to a Croatian named Drago, a man of medium build whose hair was turning gray. Drago was probably in his late thirties or early forties, although I was finding it difficult to guess the age of anyone who had gone through the war.

Seeking a place where we could talk and be undisturbed, Father Svet led us down a hill from the church into a shady grove where an old marker indicated that the Franciscans had built their first church here in 1884. We sat on two benches, with Father Svet acting as interpreter. As Drago recalled the events of the recent past, he made a strong effort to keep his emotions under control. He came from a mountain village up north, about halfway between Zenica and Sarajevo, named Kraljeva Sutjeska. On our map it was so small it was barely visible, but it was Drago's home. Once, it had been the seat of a king (which was what its name meant)—a great king, apparently, judging from Drago's reaction. And he should know: he was a professor of history and Latin at the large high school in Kakanj, the nearest town of any size. In Bosnia, as elsewhere in Europe, some high-school teachers were referred to as professor, out of respect.

Pride of heritage ran deep in Drago and presumably in everyone else of that region. He gave us one more piece of historical information: Since the time of the kings in the Middle Ages, there had been a Catholic presence in the town of about thirteen thousand, and they had preserved the folk costumes of that time. This included the distinctive black veil on the hats of the women, worn in remembrance of the last monarch of Bosnia, Queen Katerina, who went into exile in Rome when the Ottoman Turks invaded her country five centuries ago.

The more Bosnians I met, the more I realized how deeply their pride and sense of place ran. In America, we are a mostly mobile population. According to direct-mail experts, in any given year fully a quarter of us move. I tried to think of any Americans I knew who had stayed put for three generations. I couldn't. When I lived in New York City, of all the people I met, my wife was the only one who actually had been born there. Before we moved to Cape Cod, we had lived in New York, Toronto, and Princeton—all in seven years.

But in Bosnia it was common for people to live in the same village or town for so many generations that when asked how long their family had lived there, villagers would look surprised and simply say, "Always." Such continuity explains why being forcibly driven from their homes would leave a deeper wound than we could imagine, as well as why they so longed to go back, why they would want at least to be buried there.

Drago had a good life before the war. His students included Serbs, Muslims, and Croats, and while he taught a number of classes, he never had more than thirty in his classroom. As workers, his students were conscientious and happy; the majority of their fathers worked in the local coal mines.

No one in Kakanj believed this preposterous war would actually come to them. So when it did in 1993, they were completely unprepared psychologically, which was actually harder on them than being physically unready. What was worse, when the attack came, it was from Muslims, not Serbs. The 7th Muslim Brigade were ultranationalists, to be sure, and none of the Muslims with whom the Croats had lived side by side all their lives were members. But once the shooting began, it didn't matter whether you had been friends or neighbors; if you were Croatian, you were the enemy.

By no accident the attack came on the Feast of St. Anthony, a major feastday for Croatians, all of whom could be counted on to be in church. When it began, and they realized they were being ethnically cleansed, Drago was given the responsibility of getting the women and children to safety. He called on UNPROFOR (the United Nations Protection Force) for help, but the organization could do very little at the time. Somehow Drago and others managed to transport the women and children in a number of convoys to Capljina and Stolac in the heart of Croatian Hercegovina, where they would be safe.

The memory that would always remain the sharpest for him was that of leading his own children to safety. Their house was on the edge of no man's land, and the only way to safety that lay in the direction of Vares was through the woods. They started, but all at once it seemed as though people were shooting at them from all directions. Drago told his children to get *down*! Lie absolutely flat, hug the ground! They did, and they could hear the bullets zipping through the air above them like angry bees.

But they could not stay there indefinitely. So Drago showed them how to crawl on their stomachs, elbow by elbow. The progress was slow and painful—a hundred yards, two hundred. . . . The children were terrified; the youngest, eighteen months old, had to be half-pulled along.

They were sobbing, and their cries were drawing the fire of whoever was shooting at them.

Bullets were striking everywhere—on trees above their heads, on the ground next to them—but none of Drago's family was touched. Finally, after more than a mile, they cleared the woods and were safe. They were scratched and scraped, but no one was seriously hurt. It was God who did that, Drago said. So many others who had tried similar escape routes had been killed or wounded.

But as hard as escaping had been, worse was trying to adjust to being away from where their family had lived for thirteen hundred years. Being a teacher of history only aggravated the open wound; were it not for his faith, he said, he might well have gone completely to pieces. Looking into his eyes, I could see he was not exaggerating.

He seemed fairly close to the edge even now.

He said that the transition had been even harder on his wife. At least Drago had a job to go to, working in the archives of the library. It was nothing near his previous job, but it brought in a little money and got him out of the house and gave him people to talk to. His wife had no one—except the women in her weekly prayer group.

Until a week ago, Drago had looked forward to his family's returning home. There had been peace now for five months, and their return was part of the Dayton Peace Accords. But last week he had gone back—and received a shock. It was not that their home had been partially burned and destroyed, or that his parents' home had been razed to the ground, as had most of the older houses. Nor was it the reception given him by his former neighbors and students who were now in the Muslim military and police; actually they had all been friendly and respectful.

It was what he learned from some of the old Croats who

had stayed there, of whom there were now fewer than a thousand. Twelve thousand Croats had been driven out. The Bosnian president, Alija Isetbegovic, who professed to be for a return to the integrated, multi-ethnic ways of prewar Bosnia, had sent an elite unit of Muslims there, the Black Eagles. Because they were under his personal command, the police could not touch them. They had one mission: make sure no Croats returned.

Because the town no longer had a school program for Croatian children, no Croatian parents of school-age youngsters wanted to live there anymore. To me, the implication was that they would no longer have employment for a Croatian professor of history and Latin, but Drago was undeterred. He still hoped to return one day, if only to work for his neighbors and work on his property and live the remainder of his days in the seat of a king.

"Our faith does not allow us to hate," said Drago. "We don't hate our neighbor who is of another faith and another nation. If he doesn't hate us, and if we can come to appreciate each other, then there is hope for reconciliation. Someone should be held responsible for the evil that was done, but as believers, we are ready to forgive."

The words were right; whether his heart would ever match them remained to be seen.

But after we had said good-bye, I wondered: *If I had led my family to safety on their stomachs, if it had been my family's and friends' homes that had been burned down, would I even be able to pay lip service to reconciliation?*

Twilight was gathering; the trees were losing their color and becoming dark silhouettes as Father Svet walked us back to our car. Catching his cheerful visage, I thought at first that he had not been aged by the war. But he had. The gray eyes were different. They were still full of compassion, still had a twinkle, but there was a knowing in them now, a sadness that had not been there before.

We talked about peace for Bosnia. "Two things cause war," said Father Svet. "Economy and religion. When people are well off, they don't feel like risking everything they have in a war. But if they have very little and are very angry, then they may be ready to go to war."

He watched the headlights of a car going down the winding road toward the valley. "Religion is the thing that holds them in check: accountability to God."

Under more than forty years of Communism, he explained, churchgoing was regarded as socially undesirable and strongly discouraged. While some risked persecution and fought to hold onto their faith, others discarded it as no longer useful and certainly no longer fashionable.

And so a generation was born and grew up without God and without any sense that one day they would have to answer for their acts. These people became the instruments of unleashing unspeakable hatred, and they were capable of acts so obscene that others simply could not conceive of them.

"The more people go to church," Father Svet concluded, "the less likely they are to go to war." He smiled. "That was true before this war, and it will be true again. In the meantime, the only peace that will last is a strong peace. Those who would like to go back to war must know that they cannot. The economy must be rebuilt, but that will take years, not months. If IFOR[8] goes, peace goes."

---

[8] The Implementation Forces, sent by NATO to implement the Dayton Peace Accords.

He paused and smiled. "But I am absolutely optimistic, because I think the world is sick of war."

I had to ask him, "Father Svet, are you able to forgive the war-makers, including the ones who've done the atrocities?"

"I do not hate the people who have done such things," he said. "When I hear of them, I am sad. And sorry for them: to do such evil is truly a sickness of the mind—an illness and a terrible confusion. When they have their ultimate encounter with the Lord, they are going to have to answer for them. And thank God, I don't have to be there!"

It was getting late, but I was loathe to leave this friend whom I had not seen for several years and might not see for several more. I remembered when during the war I had feared I would never see him again. That had been a hard time for all of his friends, who were beyond number.

Recalling it, I realized that this might be my last opportunity to get a firsthand account of what actually did happen, before the events became inextricably woven into the tapestry of legend growing up around him.

In 1992, Father Svet had been chaplain at Bijelo Polje, the motherhouse of all the Franciscan convents in Hercegovina. It was a tiny village, too small to be on the map, located near the town of Potoci, just north of Mostar on the road to Sarajevo. It was a fertile farming community of Serbian, Muslim, and Croatian families, about eight hundred of each. With its gardens, orchard, and outbuildings, the convent had been there for several generations, and the villagers had grown accustomed to going to the sisters for help with problems. The sisters were glad to help, no matter what religion the villager might be.

When war came to eastern Croatia, then to Dubrovnik, it was all around Bosnia, but not yet actually in the village.

But when the JNA began to build up its forces in Mostar and the paramilitaries arrived, the writing was on the wall. Soon checkpoints began to appear, manned by paramilitaries. Blocking the road, forcing vehicles to stop, and demanding that their drivers produce identification was an effective way of projecting authority into a region whose ownership was undecided. Even if the guards at the checkpoints let through everyone, they restricted freedom of movement and let all know who was in charge.

More checkpoints appeared, and on the summits of the mountains around Mostar, the Serbs established gun emplacements, their long-range artillery able to pinpoint targets with devastating accuracy. JNA tanks arrived, and attack helicopters took up residence at the Mostar airport. They had no provocation, no pretext. There were not even any defenders, just civilians.

Finally in March of 1992, in Sarajevo, the Serbs fired upon a peace march. The war had begun in Bosnia, and three hours to the south, the guns ringing Mostar began to roar. First to come under fire had been the university. When it was destroyed, the bombardment shifted to the hospital, then to the schools, and then the churches. Every institution that played a key role in holding together the fabric of society was marked for destruction.

Since the convents and monasteries would be the next targets, the Franciscan provincial now directed that all the young and very elderly sisters be evacuated immediately to their house on the coast. The middle-aged sisters were allowed to remain, if that was their decision. It was an arduous journey to the coast, during which one eighty-five-year-old sister from the Mostar convent died. Two other sisters from that convent drove to Bijelo Polje to make funeral arrangements. On their return, they were stopped at a checkpoint at a gas station. They were unconcerned; they were wearing their habits and had been stopped there before.

But this time the paramilitary who had asked to see the registration did not return it. Instead, he also asked for the keys, to inspect the trunk, he said. The sister driving told him the trunk was not locked, but he demanded the keys anyway. Then with obscene gestures and remarks his partner ordered the sisters out of the car. The first paramilitary got in it and drove it to the makeshift guardhouse, where he parked it.

Badly shaken, the sisters were speechless. Another soldier, having observed what had happened, came over to them and said not unkindly, "Sisters, you have a problem. You need a lift."

"No, we don't," replied the sister who had been driving, "our car is right over there."

"That *was* your car. Now you need a lift. C'mon, I'll give you a ride home."

After that incident, the villagers of Bijelo Polje put up their own roadblocks at either end of the village. But when General Peresic, commander of the JNA in Mostar, heard of this, he was enraged. He gave them an ultimatum: Dismantle their roadblocks immediately, or he would pulverize their village. They didn't, and he did.

At the first shells, Father Svet gathered the nineteen sisters into the basement. The first explosions were terrifying, but after a while they grew used to them. By the shells' incoming whistle the sisters could even tell how close they were. Because going to their little church for Mass would be too dangerous, Father Svet decided they would use their basement chapel. On April 27, just before supper, as he was about to celebrate Mass there, a rocket grenade scored a direct hit. It came in a window on the main floor, went down through the floor into the basement chapel, and went through an inner wall into the adjacent room, where it exploded.

They all should have been killed. In Sarajevo, a similar rocket had killed fifty-three people standing in a breadline. But this one landed in a great stone sink used for flower arranging. And so, though it blew down the interior wall, its initial blast was contained. Its incendiary elements were not, however, and now the convent started to burn furiously.

Once Father Svet had gotten the sisters outside, he counted heads. The three oldest were not there. Flames were now belching from the windows, yet without hesitation he went back in. It was impossible to see through the thick, acrid smoke, but he knew the way by heart. One by one he located the three sisters and led them to safety.

The bombardment was continuous now. But whenever an approaching shell's whistle was not too near, the sisters rushed about, fetching water to fight the fire. All except Sister Elizabeth, their superior, who remained perfectly calm. So unperturbed was she, that Father Svet was concerned that something must be wrong: this century-old building was the heart of their tradition.

He shouted at her, "Don't you see the convent is on fire?"

She nodded but gave no further response. And later, thinking about it, he admired her. When the war began, they knew they might lose the house. The main thing was, they had not lost any sisters. So what was to be gained by her acting in a desperate manner? She only would have transmitted fear to the sisters who were looking to her for leadership. By remaining calm, she would not spread panic.

They soon realized that they could not stop this fire, nor was there any point in standing around watching it. In the village Father Svet arranged for temporary shelter for most of the sisters, but not for the three oldest who had been caught in the fire. He could see that they had been badly unnerved by their experience; in no way could they go through another bombardment.

The only thing to do was to get them out of Bijelo Polje. And there was only one safe, quiet place for them: the convent at Siroki Brijeg, an hour away. He could not go in daylight; he would never make it past the snipers. They would have to go at night, without lights. Crossing the bridge would be the tricky part; once they reached the mountain, Father Svet knew a steep track used only by hunters with four-wheel-drive vehicles. The Serbs were not from the area; they would not know of the track and would never think of looking for him there.

Somehow his white Volkswagen Golf had survived the bombardment intact. He rolled down the windows so a sniper's bullet would not send glass flying and disconnected the brake lights, which might give away their position. The sky was overcast, which would help, but at that moment, he would have preferred a black car. They waited for nightfall.

Half an hour before dark, he started the engine and left it running, so that later the noise of the starter would not draw the attention of anyone across the river who might be listening.

It was time. He signaled the sisters to be as quiet as possible as they got in, then gently shut the door after them. Getting in his own side, he shifted, gently engaged the clutch, and started rolling. Everything in him wanted to gun the car for the bridge, but he forced himself to go slowly.

They were over the bridge before the first shots were fired at them. Father Svet jammed the accelerator to the floor, plunging into the brush on the side of the mountain. A huge military searchlight atop the adjacent mountain switched on and started looking for them. Father Svet stopped behind a thick bush. The light came near, then went away, then came back again. Finally it switched off. Still he waited long enough to give the men manning the searchlight time to relax and slip back into boredom. Then, easing the car into gear, he crept up the track and over the shoulder of the mountain. They were safe!

Driving over the rest of the dirt track without lights, it took them three hours to reach Siroki Brijeg. When they arrived, the emotionally exhausted nuns were taken inside. Father Svet turned the car around and headed back for more sisters—and disappeared.

A day went by. Two. In America, we learned from Sister Janja that Father Svet was missing; for some reason her phone kept working throughout the war. It was the only line I knew of in Mostar or Medjugorje that never had a problem. Each night Sister Isabel in Steubenville, Ohio, would call me, or I would call her to get an update, which we would relay to the fax network.

Sister Janja was like a blood sister to Father Svet. When she first had heard he was missing after his rescue of the nuns, she had laughed. "Sometimes—*no*, all the time—I think Svet has too much courage!" After two days with no word, Sister Janja was not laughing. She asked all their friends in America to please pray.

As the third day dawned with still no word, I began to fear the worst. Ever since my conversation with Father Svet on the rocky hill on the eve of the war, I had suspected that he might be martyred. Once the war had begun, the man had no fear. When the friars of his former monastery in Konjic were being held hostage, it was he who went through the lines to bring them food and word from the outside world.

When refugees in Makarska on the coast needed food, it was he who went to Glavaticevo, bought a farmer friend's entire harvest of cabbages *and* his truck in which to haul them, and drove them down to the coast. So familiar had he become to the guards at Serb or Muslim checkpoints that they just waved through the crazy brown-robe. He had pushed the envelope so many times that I was afraid he might get ahead of God's timetable for him.

Now it appeared that he had. When I suddenly came undone thinking about it, a friend helped: "If he *is* called to make the ultimate sacrifice, then it will be the completion of God's plan for him. You must release him to it."

More hours past. Each time the phone rang, I snatched it up, half dreading what it might convey. Finally on the third day, there was a call from Father Slavko Soldo, pastor of St. Cyril and Methodius Church in New York. Father Svet had once served under him and always used St. Cyril's as home base when he came to America. "He's all right!" Father Slavko exclaimed. "He just called! He's back at Siroki Brijeg. He had car trouble. I told him, 'Sveto, stay put! I want to pray *with* you, not *to* you!'"

Many people rejoiced greatly that day.

So what had actually happened?

The track was very rough, Father Svet explained. A rock had punctured the fuel line, and he had no way to fix it. He was a long way from anywhere, and when he did come to a dwelling, the phone, like practically everyone's, was out of order. Eventually he found a friendly military unit, and they radioed for help. It had never occurred to him that anyone might be worried.

SEVEN

BOULEVARD OF BROKEN TREES

Mostar — The sky was leaden gray the day we got our first close-up look at the war's devastation. This was the first non-picture-perfect day since our arrival, and it fit. We were parked on the tree-shaded, divided boulevard that paralleled the Neretva River and had once been the pride of Mostar. Across the street was a scene unlike any I had ever witnessed: a broad vista of ruin, huge mounds of broken brick and twisted metal. It stretched for more than a mile along the boulevard and extended in depth all the way to the river. Here and there a lone wall was still standing, imprinted with what it had contained—stairways, bathrooms, even wallpaper.

Reaching back for something with which to compare it, I recalled news clips of condemned buildings being demolished. With carefully placed charges, demolition experts had collapsed the buildings in upon themselves. When the dust cleared, all that was left was a great heap of rubble. But to equal this wasteland would take thirty or forty of such buildings.

Then I remembered photographs of the results of saturation bombing during World War II. They were exactly like this, even to the point of being in black-and-white. For there was no color here: the brick-beige and cement-gray rubble blended with the slate-gray sky. It was as if someone had turned the color knob on the television set all the way to off.

I was appalled. Heightening the effect was the vivid, fresh memory of Medjugorje, where the colors had been so rich and luminous. There we had been surrounded by love; here, all color had been leached out of the scene as we surveyed the ashes of hate. In fifteen miles we had journeyed from the edge of Heaven to the edge of Hell.

At the front edge of the nearest pile was a clump of bricks still stuck together. They seemed to have been part of a corner. I thought about the work that had gone into the building's construction: skilled masons working on a scaffolding, expertly laying the bricks, seaming them with mortar, constantly checking them against the stretched string, tapping them into alignment with the heels of their trowels. Day after day the wall had grown like a living thing, slowing as they framed a window, accelerating as they reached the top.

I thought of what had gone before: the vision that someone first had had for the building, the architect who had shown how the vision could become a reality, the draftsman who had drawn the blueprints that guided the masons. And I thought of what had come after: the first families moving into their new home, and then the generations growing up there, each imparting a layer to the living building's personality.

And then I thought of the casual ease with which it had been destroyed. Atop each of the nearby mountains was a crew manning a long-range gun. It took a strong man to lift, carry, and load the shell of such a gun, but that round of ammunition, costing maybe a thousand dollars, could blow a hole in a brick wall as wide as a man's outstretched arms.

Once the wall was breached, the destruction attracted the attention of gunners on other hills, like wolves scenting the blood of a wounded animal. The gunners attacked the building again and again, opening one hole after another.

Finally, when the building was mortally stricken with its entrails exposed and steam and water bleeding from gaping wounds, the gunners engaged in a contest to see which gun would bring it down. They accelerated the pace of their firing as the end drew near, until with a great crash and a cloud of dust and a cheer from the victorious crew, the building died.

But the gunners were not sated. Concentrating now on any walls still standing, they knocked them down, too, until at last everything was flattened. The entire killing process would take less than an hour.

Anyone looking at these remains, probing them with a toe, would be compelled to ask: Why? What was the point of such malevolent destruction? If you were the gunner—or the battery captain, or the commander of artillery, or the commander-in-chief of all forces in the sector, or the supreme commander of the army—why did you do it?

There was only one possibility: to take something away from the people you hated, something that they loved, or at least found useful. Why did you hate them?

Because of the terrible things their grandparents had done to our grandparents. Because of the terrible things their soldiers had done to our soldiers.

But these apartment buildings were the homes of civilians who had never done anything to anyone. Why kill them and ruin their lives?

They were different from us. They had nicer things than we had. They thought they were better than us.

Who? That family of six, who lived in #3B? The one

where both the husband and wife had to work, with an old grandmother and three kids in school? That family who could barely afford their rent and were lucky to get meat once a week?

Listen, you can't afford to think of them as individuals. They're the enemy—all of them. They deserve what they're getting.

Why?

Because of what they did to us in the past.

How far in the past?

During the war.

Which war?

The Second World War. They had concentration camps, too, you know; we did not invent genocide.

But you weren't even alive then.

That's all right; I heard about it.

Where will it end?

Not with me.

When this is over, what will you have accomplished?

When this is over, our people will be safe, and we will have what we need.

Is it right to take from another?

They did it to us. And they would again, if they could.

It was pointless, I saw, to argue right or wrong. Pointless to apportion blame. Pointless to assert that the Serbs did this, or the Croats that, or the Muslims the other. Pointless to try to convict the wrongdoer in the court of world opinion or to try to soften his heart, that he might become sorry for what he had done. In his eyes he would always be the victim, wrongfully accused and misunderstood.

I looked along the boulevard that had later become the deadline between the Croats and the Muslims. Anyone crossing here could be killed by snipers from either side. And their bodies would lie there for days, because anyone trying to remove them would be killed.

But the most poignant image of the boulevard was not the desolation and ruin; it was what had become of the trees.

This was one of the streets on which I had walked with Father Svet on that cold, crisp morning just before the war. There had been chips of mica in the sidewalk that had glistened in the sunlight like a field of tiny diamonds. And the grand old shade trees had seemed like the courtly gentlemen lining the Bois de Boulogne.

I looked at them now with a tightening in my throat. They had lost all of their limbs in the bombardment. They were only trunks now, seven or eight feet tall, standing in line along the edge of the sidewalk like silent mourners. But their root systems had remained intact, and so with the coming of spring, life once again had surged up their capillaries to put out a new growth of leaves. The barren trunks suddenly sprouted leaves everywhere. And now each trunk wore a thick green coat of leaves, from which an occasional dead limb reached heavenward, as if in appeal.

"Don't go there!" our guide Nada called out to Luke, who was on the other side of the street, moving in past some shrubs to take a close-up picture of wreckage from a former infirmary. "It could be mined! There are still mines everywhere; it's best to stay on the pavement."

Luke moved back toward the street, and I turned back to the mountain of rubble.

The war-makers have their belief system, too. It begins with the German philosopher, Nietzsche, who said the world is divided into *Übermenschen* and *Untermenschen,* masters and slaves. Those called to be the master race must fulfill their destiny.

Even if to do so is not right?

As the medieval German poet Walther observed: Might *is* right.

And God?

In the words of the German warrior-king, Frederick the Great, God is on the side of the heavy battalions.

I shook my head; it was pointless to go on. Such thinking was corrupt beyond redemption, but what had caused it? Power tends to corrupt, wrote Lord Acton a century ago to his friend, Bishop Creighton, and absolute power corrupts absolutely. A schoolyard bully perceives that he has absolute power. There is no one else as strong as he, no one who dares stand up to him. Nor is there any accountability. During recess, the teacher is indoors, and the bully is free to do whatever he wants, to whomever he chooses.

The only thing that can make a bully stop is the arrival of someone stronger. Until then, he will strut and stick out his chest, intimidating and humiliating every kid in the school. He is compelled to: the perception that he has power needs constant reinforcement.

Can his heart be changed? Only if it can still be reached by God. A heart in communion with God is slow to anger, quick to forgive. It remains soft and malleable; God can shape it and reshape it—make it a slim, elegant pitcher to pour out love, or a fat, round bowl to receive it.

As long as a heart is not completely cut off from God, it can be softened. The war-maker wants to harden. From such hearts come not love but lust—for revenge, gratification, power. A hardened heart pours a bitter brew that leaves behind a stain and a sour residue. Humanity can develop a taste for such a tea, so the sweet savor of God's potion becomes abhorrent.

"We need to go soon," Nada called. I nodded.

Many hearts had already been lost, hardened into hatred

and endless revenge. Many more were on the verge of join-ing them; the kiln's fire was hot, its door open.

"C'mon, let's go!" called Luke from the car, and I hur-ried to join them.

EIGHT

POWER TO LOVE

Mostar — We had heard about a church in Mostar that reached out to Serbs, Muslims, and Croats alike. It was not just rumor; we had actually met church members of all three nationalities. Here finally we found a return to harmony among the three ethnic groups. They were Bosnians again, but as they said, they were first Christians. And they truly cared for one another. This was so unusual—*they* were so unusual—that I wanted to meet the founding pastor of this church, Nikola Skrinjaric.

One look around the two-bedroom, second-floor walk-up of Nikola and Sandra Skrinjaric told me it was too small to keep neat. Their two infant daughters vied constantly for Sandra's undivided attention, and she had her hands full. Nikola's love for all of them went without saying, but he looked as if he would not resent a business interruption that would require him to be elsewhere. In other words, except for their language, it was situation normal for most working-class American households.

That is, until Nikola and Sandra got to the heart of what compelled them. Then, transformed by the depth and clarity of their vision, this everyday setting became out of the ordinary. I had the eerie feeling of being in the remote mountain fastness in a Latin American jungle, listening to two leaders of a revolution as they described their vision of their country's future. Though their followers were as yet few in number, their commitment was absolute. Watching them and listening to them, I had the distinct feeling that their vision might indeed come to pass.

Nikola even looked and acted the part. He had a penetrating gaze that quickly took the measure of a stranger. Before entering the ministry full-time, he had been a long-haul trucker, an occupation that, I sensed, well suited his restless nature. Patience did not appear to be his strong suit, nor did he, I imagined, suffer fools (and dilettantes) graciously. I never saw him actually lose his temper, but I could imagine that it was not a pretty sight. That he was now a missionary was ironic and somehow fitting because he was dependent on outside support—a role in which he could not afford to be impatient with anyone. Fortunately he also possessed tremendous self-discipline.

His wife Sandra had a smooth, open, Slavic face which was at once plain and strikingly beautiful. Together they made an arresting couple, though it would be more accurate to call them a team, for here was truly a case of one plus one equaling more than two. Fluent in English, Sandra acted as Nikola's interpreter. He had, I suspected, a fair grasp of English himself, but like other leaders, he preferred to use an interpreter. The built-in delay that translating required was often useful when it came to formulating a response to a difficult question. With a personality that was as strong as her husband's, Sandra was highly articulate in her own right. When her interpretations into English ran twice as long as his replies, it was obvious that she was elaborating and obvious that he approved.

As the fighting in Mostar reached its heaviest phase, they

were both in Zagreb. One day, a Christian friend invited Nikola to come to Mostar to help with the humanitarian aid work there, and he was about to accept when suddenly he had his entire family to look after. Sandra elaborated. When the Serbs invaded Croatia, they cleansed his family's village of Okukani near Nova Gradiska. One day to his complete surprise, his mother and father and eleven other relatives arrived on his doorstep. Giving them his two-room apartment, he moved in with friends, then set about helping them become situated. "God took amazing care of my family," he said. "It was a miracle they all found jobs, and my parents found a small cottage in a peaceful area outside Zagreb."

He went to Mostar just before Christmas 1992. One morning he woke up, absolutely sure in his heart that God wanted him in Mostar. It was Christmas morning. He called Sandra and told her. "He invited me to marry him," she added, "and to come spend New Year's in Mostar. I told him it would be wiser for him to return to Zagreb, since such things can be emotional, and, you know, we could talk about it."

He did come back, but soon they married, and with the help of a British organization called Spring Harvest, they headed permanently for Mostar. They almost didn't make it. In March 1993, they were driving through Jablanica, south of Konjic, at the moment that the Muslims and Croats turned on each other. Suddenly they were pinned down in a battle zone with people being killed all around them—eighteen in all. But they emerged unhurt. They settled in Mostar and began raising a church and, a year later, a family.

From the beginning Nikola had decided that the best way to win people to Christ was to live as a Christian and let his life speak for itself. Then if anyone asked why he did what he did, he would feel free to tell them. In an age of endless talk, it was an unusual form of evangelism, though hardly unprecedented, I thought, recalling Father Svet. It *was* unusual in Nikola's new line of work: overseeing the distribution of aid for the international, all-volunteer relief agency, known as Agape.

In relief work, one deals with food and clothing and heating fuel—things that can literally make the difference between survival and death for a starving, freezing populace. Nikola was scrupulously fair and honest, and he required the same high standard from those who worked with him. Bad apples, and there were a few, were soon weeded out.

He was also scrupulously impartial. The various ethnic relief agencies tended to look after their own kind, but he emphasized to his workers that they were to look after *all* kinds. Gradually Agape gained a reputation for rectitude and evenhandedness, as well as the inspired, selfless love that its title embodied. This agape love began to draw people of all three ethnic groups to the place where the workers worshiped.

Some people *did* join the church for the wrong reasons. At the distribution center, if there was a long line when they were handing out food parcels, a new member might say, "Now that I am a member of the church, may I stand first in line?"

"No," Nikola would tell him, "now that you are a member, you must stand at the end of the line. And when you get your parcel, you must share it with someone else. Because that's what Jesus would do."

At that, some had left. But others changed.

After three years, the church was not so little anymore. There were more than one hundred baptized members, and the mix was evenly split. Whenever a stranger would ask Nikola why he did what he did, he would share the burden on his heart: forgiveness did not come from the outside.

Each person had to be changed from the inside, and only God could do that. No one could forgive until he or she had God's peace inside.

"Nikola," I asked him, "reconciliation seems to be the current buzz-word in Bosnia. I mean, all sorts of groups and business consultants, even experts on conflict resolution, are coming over here from the States, all excited about helping to rehab Bosnia. What do you think about them?"

He nodded and shot off an answer, which I was sure Sandra tidied up in the translation. "These people set up their workshops and bring young people together for sporting or social or cultural events. They mean well. But the Communists did the same sort of thing with no lasting success."

"Did anyone object to the fact that Agape has a religious orientation?"

He nodded before Sandra finished translating, which confirmed my suspicion that he at least understood English.

There were people, he explained, who wanted all relief and humanitarian aid distributed by nonreligious organizations such as the Red Cross, but they missed the point. You could feed a starving man and temporarily satisfy his physical hunger. But unless you also satisfied his spiritual hunger, he would only become hungry again and ready to go back to war. Without forgiveness, there could be no reconciliation. And only God could enable forgiveness.

Psychiatrists and psychologists claimed that time was all they needed. Give them enough time, and the deepest wounds would heal. But what happened after World War II put the lie to that. The hard evidence was that the majority of people hurt by their neighbors *never* forgave them. No matter how much time passed—even forty-three years.

"Let me ask you something," Nikola challenged. "If someone invades your land, kills your children, rapes your wife—what would you need to be able to forgive?"

I already knew the answer, because I had already asked myself the same question. "A miracle," I murmured.

"Two of them," observed Sandra.

"I know," Nikola said, "that Jesus is the *only* one who can heal such wounds. No setting up of partitions, no human effort can make your heart able to forgive."

He stood up. "I am convinced that our personal relationship with God is what matters!" he exclaimed. "If I really have a relationship with Him, He will give me the power to forgive. He will give me the power to love those whom I have every reason in the world to hate."

Fired by what he was saying, he raced on, and Sandra was hard-pressed to keep up. "We haven't stopped with Mostar. There is a need for this forgiveness all over Bosnia. [All over the world, added Sandra.] God has given us a vision, that this is part of what He has called us to do."

During the war, when the shelling made venturing outside dangerous for anyone, Nikola's work constantly required him to travel to different parts of the city. Each time he left home, he was not sure he would see his wife and children again. After several close calls, Nikola began to sense that God was keeping him alive, so that he could bring a light to other people's lives.

When we said good-bye, I wondered if I would ever see him again. Probably not, unless I came back to Bosnia. But I did expect to hear of him. His movement might be growing slowly, but it *was* growing, and I imagined one day a great many people would hear of him.

I did know that I would think of him again. In fact, whenever the subject of surrendering to God came up in my mind, he was on the short list of those of whom I would be reminded.

NINE

JASMINA

Osijek — Eight days later, at a seminary in Osijek in eastern Croatia, I met one more person from the little church in Mostar that was home to people of all three backgrounds. She was a Muslim artist named Jasmina. Thin, blond, and in her early thirties, she had the same sadness in the corners of her eyes as so many who had endured the bombardment. She was well educated, and her English, though awkward at times, was perfectly understandable. She also had a nervous apprehension, like a doe in the forest who had already been shot at.

When the shells starting falling on Mostar in April 1992, Jasmina, her husband, and their one-year-old son were living in her parents' apartment. Her father, a cultural Muslim, had once worked for the JNA as a civilian and had retired to Belgrade with his wife, who was also Muslim. They had left their apartment to their daughter and her family. The problem was, their apartment building had once been the JNA's and was located in what was now the Croatian sector of that city. Most of the JNA staff had been Serbs and, to make matters worse, so was Jasmina's husband.

What they could expect for the duration soon became vividly clear when a group of Croatian soldiers stomped into the apartment and searched the place. Disappointed at not finding anything incriminating, the soldiers accused them of being connected with the JNA, because they were in that building. Jasmina's husband, badly shaken by the episode, was anxious to get his family out of Mostar; he could almost feel the hatred coming through the walls.

But, Jasmina argued, where would they go? She did not want to go to her parents in Belgrade, or to his, either. And they didn't know anyone anywhere else other than two cousins of his in Switzerland. They argued a lot as the shelling intensified. They spent more and more time in the apartment, with only Jasmina occasionally going out to try to find some food. The rest of the time they listened to the explosions and fought.

Finally as the bombardment came close enough to rattle their windows, her husband could take it no longer. He bundled Jasmina and their son Tibor into the car of a friend, who drove them to a refugee camp on the coast. But there, instead of things being better, they were much worse. Somehow the refugees who were Croats found out that Jasmina was married to a Serb. They shunned her and were unmercifully cruel to her.

A few days later she learned that her husband had been taken prisoner by the Croats. That settled it: she was going back. Taking little Tibor with her, she returned to Mostar and went to the authorities, first to the police station, then to the prison, to see if she could get them to release her husband. She made these trips with her son in tow, right through the grenading, because she had the strangest feeling that God was protecting them. The feeling was strengthened when a grenade went off practically beside them. They should have been killed, but they weren't even scratched. She wrote her husband, "I'm sure God is protecting Tibor, and somehow us, too, because we are with Him. When you are in a really dangerous situation, think about Tibor, and know that God is with Him. In that way you will go in this protection of God."

Two weeks later, there was another prisoner exchange. Her husband was taken to the front line and offered a chance to go over to the Serb side, as he had Serb parents and two Serb brothers already on that side. But Jasmina would not leave Mostar. He pleaded with her: they had family over there. But she said that if she ever did leave Mostar, it would be to go somewhere far away from former Yugoslavia, someplace where there were no Serbs, Muslims, or Croats.

When he was finally released, he rejoined them in their apartment. And he was miserable. In prison, he had been with other Serbs who were friendly to him, but now he could feel the hatred of those around them, and he waited for the inevitable, the day that they would come to take out their vengeance on him. Jasmina continued to be the one to go out for food, but it was becoming harder and harder to find any. She could not go to the Muslim relief agency, Merhamet, because she and her family were not really Muslims. Nor could she go to the Catholic agency, Caritas; they weren't Catholics, either. They weren't anything.

But then a strange thing happened: someone came to them and gave them some boxes of baby food for Tibor. After making sure they saved enough for him, they were so hungry they ate some themselves. They never did find out who the strangers were.

Confined to the apartment with no food, they were at each other constantly now. They did have cigarettes; a friend of theirs had joined the Croatian army and kept them well supplied. But they had nothing to do but smoke and fight.

Then they learned that Norway was taking refugees

without any special documents. Norway was open; they would go there. But how to get there? They would have to sell everything they owned to buy the tickets. And as there was no law enforcement anymore, selling on the street had become exceedingly dangerous; people just took what you were trying to sell, and there was nothing you could do about it. Besides, everybody was trying to sell something; even if they were able to sell their possessions, the price would be so low, it would not be nearly enough.

Then her husband remembered his cousins in Switzerland. He would call them and ask them to lend him the money for the tickets. But where would they find a telephone? There were few lines in Mostar that were still working, but he had heard of a man who worked for humanitarian aid and who did have a phone that worked and would let them use it. They went to find him.

It was late in the afternoon and dark when they left the apartment, and now they were scared, because they had also heard that the man was a Croat from Zagreb. They thought, *When he realizes we're not Croatian, maybe he won't help us. Maybe it's dangerous to tell him.* But they had no other options; they decided to tell him.

They knocked on his door. When he opened it, they blurted out who they were and how they wanted to go to Norway and why they wanted to use the phone. And then they were shocked when he smiled, invited them in, showed them the phone, and said, "There it is. Use it any time you want."

But he did even more. He went to his refrigerator and gave them food—not only some of what was there, but all that he had. They were stunned. "It's too much," Jasmina gasped. "Think of yourself."

"It's not my food," he smiled. "It's God's food."

Well, whoever's food it was, she was not about to turn it down, not with three mouths to feed.

When they were unable to reach anyone in Switzerland that night, their host said, "Look, come back any time; it's open to you." They talked a little, and he told them that he worked at Agape and was looking forward to his fiancée coming soon, and that they would probably be married here. If they were ever interested, he said as they said good-bye, they would be welcome at his church which was not far from where they lived. His name was Nikola Skrinjaric.

Jasmina and her husband were both touched by his kindness, and that evening at home, they talked about him. As they did, Jasmina realized it was the first conversation she had had about something good since the war had begun. Then they ate some of his food. She could not get over it. In all this desert, when they had been hungry for so long, when Tibor had been crying and there had been nothing to give him, now suddenly to have food—and not just food, but milk and butter and jam! She started to cry. It was another miracle, she decided, like the strangers who had brought the boxes of baby food and the grenade that should have killed them but hadn't.

So the three of them went to this man's church on Sunday afternoon and listened to him talk about God and read about Him from the Bible. As Jasmina listened, she felt peace in her heart, something she hadn't felt since even before the war started. Nikola gave her a copy of the Bible, and when they got home, she said to her husband, "Well, here's the Bible; now we can start our life over, with the Bible in it."

But pretty soon they were fighting again, and before long the fighting was worse than ever, until she could no longer remember what they'd had between them in the beginning.

It was as bad as a marriage could be. Crying, she shouted at him, "We're not even like a couple anymore!" Then she went and found the Bible and said, "We'll take this Bible, and we'll ask God, and God will lead us, and it will be all right." But her husband wasn't interested.

Then when things could not possibly get any worse, they grew a little better. They reached a cousin in Switzerland who said he would send all the money they needed. They were going to Norway!

But Jasmina was not excited. She did not want to leave, but she was too ashamed to say anything. Here her husband had been in prison, and now he was free, and they could go far away to a beautiful country—how could she be so ungrateful? Besides, what could she offer their son in Mostar? Nothing. So she didn't say anything as her husband, happy for the first time since the war had started, made plans for their departure. In March 1993, the money arrived, as well as the documents they would need to take with them. They would go to Croatia and from there to Norway.

On the night before their departure, Jasmina could not sleep. While her husband and Tibor slept, she sat up and had a cigarette and thought, *Why am I going to Norway? I have a bad marriage here; I am going to have the same bad marriage there. The only reason to go is for food. All my life, I have been searching for a special kind of love, and now all that's over. I am going to go eat in Norway.*

She realized she was empty, not physically, but spiritually. Before the war, she and some of her friends had tried meditation, joining a group that was led by followers of the Maharishi. It had seemed to bring peace of a sort, but in wartime it hadn't worked at all. Meditation flunked the rocket-grenade exam. Now all of her friends had left Mostar, and she was completely alone.

She hugged her knees and started to cry. "Only you, God," she murmured through her tears, not realizing what she was saying, "only you is all I have."

In that moment, in her mind very clearly she saw the name "Jesus," written in light.

"*Jesus?*" she exclaimed aloud. And then more softly, so she wouldn't wake her family, "You know who I am. My name is Jasmina. That's a Muslim name. My parents are Muslim. What should I do, change my parents?"

She was in wonder, but a little hurt and angry, too. "What connection is there with you and me, Jesus? *You* gave me Muslim parents; that wasn't *my* idea!"

And then in her heart, He answered her. She could never pretend that she did not hear Him: *Put away what other people are telling you. I am telling you that you are mine, and I am your God.*

The moment she received that word, she saw Christ on the cross before her. As she gazed at Him, in her heart she somehow knew that all those wounds were for her.

She knew about Jesus from movies and through the stories in the Bible. But she had treated the Bible like a poem— a beautiful piece of philosophy. In that moment, however, gazing at the wounds on His body and the blood, she realized that it was personal: He had gone through all of that, for her.

"Jesus," she whispered, "that happened to you—for me. You allowed it, not just for all sins, but for *my* sins!"

As she said that, she felt His assurance in her heart that it was true. Until that moment she had not realized He had died for her personal "indiscretions."

She looked at Him. "Then my first sin is that I have never in my life talked to you, Jesus. I never in my life asked you what to do. I always did it my way, in my brain. I never asked you if I should study or get married. I just figured out my life by my clever self. So that's my first sin and please forgive me."

After doing that, she realized that she needed to ask forgiveness for many other things—her whole life, in fact. With much weeping, she spent most of the night remembering things for which she needed to ask Him to forgive her, and each time He did. With His forgiveness came a new light and peace inside. She was astonished. She had never thought she could change inside. "Jesus," she said softly, "you said you are my Lord. Then here is my family—my husband, my son, and me. You know I don't want to go to Norway, but if you are my Lord, take us; I will go with you anywhere."

But now she realized she had a new problem. What was she going to do about all this? She was a Muslim. How could she tell people that Jesus was her Lord? How could she tell *anyone* that she had talked with God? She couldn't; the secret would be between her and God forever. But that night she knew in her heart the truth about Him.

The next morning, as she got ready to leave for Norway, her little boy's throat was hurting badly—so badly that she took him to the doctor. After the doctor had examined Tibor, he said that the boy had a serious infection and would have to have five days of penicillin injections. She was relieved: they would have to put off their departure for at least five more days.

But her husband had grown more fearful than ever. He was afraid that he would never get out of Mostar, and he was convinced that if he, a Serb, tried to sell the things they could not take with them, he would be killed. So when he heard that they would have to wait five more days, he said, "What would you think about my going first? I'm a man and a Serb; it will be easier for you with your Muslim name to go later and it will not be such a dangerous situation."

"Okay," she replied, "*nema problema.*"

So her husband left, and she stayed with Tibor. But during those five days the Croatian government announced new travel restrictions and that new documents would be needed. They were simply overflowing with refugees and could not process any more. She could still go, they assured her, but it was going to take more time. She could expect the special documents she would need to be sent from Zagreb in May.

Then, just before they were due to arrive, the new war broke out between the Muslims and the Croats. She would not be going anywhere. And things became even worse. The hatred that her husband had felt toward Serbs, was now directed toward Muslims. She was a Muslim living in the Croat sector in a former JNA building. She spent most of the time in the apartment, reading the Bible and talking to Jesus. And she was no longer scared, not even when soldiers came barging in to search her apartment. She was full of joy because she knew Jesus was with her and Tibor, and she praised Him so loudly that everyone knew Jesus was her Lord. To her surprise, her neighbors didn't seem to mind; in fact, several came to have her read the Bible to them. At night, she would pray, "Now, Jesus, lead us to sleep and give us peace." And He did.

Even during the worst shelling, her apartment was so peaceful that several other Muslim women who couldn't sleep in their own apartments came and asked if they could sleep on her floor. She would read the Bible to them, and they would sleep. In time, they started praying to Jesus themselves, and they joined her church.

Soon she began working at Agape, from which I first heard of her. I had made a point of looking her up when we arrived in Osijek.

"I was serving God," she said, "but at the same time He was healing me."

"That's a lovely story," I told her, "but what about your husband? He's up in Norway, but presumably you talk to him. What does he think of all of this?"

She nodded. "He was angry, at first. But then, when we talked, he began to realize the change that was happening in me, and he was happy." She smiled. "I had prayed, 'O God, turn me to my husband,' and He did. My heart has changed towards him. I can now say that I love him."

"Does that mean that you and Tibor will be going to Norway?" As much as I sympathized with her, I was a husband and a father, too; I knew how I would feel, if I were stuck in Norway without my family.

"We're going this fall, as soon as I say good-bye to my parents. I haven't seen them in five years and don't know when I'll see them again." She paused. "Now that I've been healed, God wants me together with my husband as a family. And we will be Christian parents to our son."

I wished her good luck and realized that I had hard evidence of the fruit of Nikola's ministry. That fruit, too, was good.

TEN

THE RIGHT THING

Mostar — On our last night in Mostar, Luke and I had dinner with an old friend of mine, Jozo Kraljevic, who had been my driver and interpreter here in December 1991. Four years of war had taken their toll on him. In the old days he had a rather grand style, which he carried off with *élan*. Had he a cigarette-holder, a broad-brimmed fedora, and a silk sportcoat draped over his shoulders, he would have been taken for an Italian filmmaker. (As it was, he bore a distinct resemblance to Vittorio de Sica.) But the shoulders were stooped now, the jauntiness gone. And like the others who had remained in Mostar for the duration, a sadness haunted his eyes.

Before the war he had been doing rather well in the import-export business. The only trouble was, he was being paid in Yugoslav dinars, and his savings were in a Yugoslav bank. Until five years ago, it did not matter: the dinar was steady, one of the most stable currencies of the Eastern Bloc countries. But war wrought financial havoc, as well as every other kind. To keep meeting the huge JNA payroll, the mint in Belgrade had started running its presses overtime. When we had last been together, I had been shocked to find the dollar worth sixty dinars. That was nothing, Jozo said, to what followed. In February it was two hundred, in March, six hundred. Two years later, it took twenty million dinars to buy a loaf of bread. Jozo, along with most of the middle-class population of former Yugoslavia, was financially wiped out.

But Jozo was a survivor. He had once taught English, and now he parlayed this skill (coupled with his *savoir faire)* into well-paid if sporadic assignments as an interpreter/negotiator for delegations of European Community observers or UNPROFOR detachments. At present he was working for Habena, the Herzeg-Bosnian News Agency that fed items to the various international wire services. In what little spare time remained, he was translating books.

Once during the war I had pleaded with him by phone to leave Mostar. Unlike Sarajevo, people were still able to drive out, and his twenty-year-old Volkswagen still ran. The Franciscans might have felt called to remain, but Jozo had nothing keeping him there. Why did he not take his family and run the gauntlet? Father Svet seemed to dart in and out with impunity.

"Where would I go?" Jozo replied solemnly. "There are rivers of refugees everywhere, because these terrorists don't just kill, they torture. And when they're done, it is not a clean death, as with a bullet. Their favorite way is slitting throats. No, if I am to die, I prefer to die here."

He didn't die. It was, as always, a delight to listen to him talk, and like an actor responding to a good audience, he rose to the occasion. His cigarette, held between thumb and two fingers, became a baton which he used to circumscribe and underscore. And that marvelous accent tasted like strawberries and clotted cream!

Every Bosnian had a war story: one singular, harrowing episode that would never fade. A few, like Jozo's, were uncomfortable as well as indelible in that they challenged me to look inside myself.

One evening, negotiating on behalf of the UN, Jozo had brokered a ninety-minute cease-fire between the Croats and Muslims in order to evacuate civilians from the Muslim sector. The cease-fire would commence at 8:30 P.M. and end at 10:00—time enough for three buses, escorted by UN vehicles, to cross the river to the Muslim side of the city and pick up anyone who had been trapped there and might want to come out. They would announce the cease-fire ahead of time and would use megaphones to broadcast its purpose as they drove slowly through the streets.

Hearing of the plan, an aged woman who knew Jozo made a special appeal to him: bring out her sister, who was even older than she. According to the last word she had, her sister was hiding in the basement of an apartment building that had been savagely shelled and abandoned. When her sister heard the megaphone announcement, she would think it was a trick and would refuse to come out to the buses. Would Jozo go in and bring her out himself? If he didn't, she would die, because she was so old, and there was no one over there to give her food. Without thinking, Jozo promised he would, and he took the address.

Promptly at 8:30, the Croat artillery fell silent, and small arms fire on both sides of the river ceased. But the UN convoy was tardy getting organized and underway; by the time it crossed the only remaining bridge, with Jozo's Volkswagen bringing up the rear, half the allotted time had already passed. They traveled without lights (one could never be certain a cease-fire would be honored) and with just enough moonlight by which to see. Up and down the dark streets they slowly moved, using their megaphones, trolling for refugees. In ones and twos people emerged from the shadows. They obviously suspected treachery, but as they weighed the alternative, which was to go on indefinitely living as they had been, a few and then more decided it was worth the gamble and scrambled aboard the buses.

As they rolled past the address Jozo had been given, he stopped his Volkswagen and waited, while the convoy moved into the next street. He strained to see or hear anything, but encountered only darkness. Leaving the engine running, he got out and checked his watch: ten minutes to the deadline. He would have barely enough time to do this.

The building was a hollow shell; that it was still standing was a miracle. He walked a few feet into what was once the ground floor and called out the sister's name. No answer. He walked in further, as far as he dared, then called louder— loud enough to be heard downstairs, through a closed door. He called her name, then told her who he was, and that he had come at her sister's request. He listened intently. Nothing. There were six minutes left. Shaking his head, he turned and started back to the car.

And then behind him he heard something.

Just a rat, he told himself, or a bit of the building settling. Best to get going. But he could not be sure. He hesitated, then went back in, further this time, feeling his way through the darkness. He called her name again. No answer. And no further sound. He glanced at his watch: three minutes to go. He called as loudly as he could, trying to keep the urgency out of his voice, so as not to spook her. She had to come out, right now! There was no more time! He listened, pleading with the darkness to let him hear something.

What he heard was a distant whistle and explosion at the other end of the sector. The cease-fire had ended. More explosions followed, coming nearer. He raced for the car, jumped in, and threw it into gear. Now the gunners were firing constantly, as if making up for the hour and a half they had lost. The barrage was almost upon him. He tore through the streets, hurtling around corners. Suddenly in the moon-light he could see the bridge up ahead, the buses moving across it, followed by the white UN vehicle.

All hell was breaking loose behind him, as he jammed the accelerator to the floor, careening towards the bridge. The explosions were almost beside him, as if they were racing him to see who would reach the bridge first. Jozo won. But as he swerved onto the bridge, he almost lost it, fighting to keep the old car under control. A shell burst in the road behind him, where he had been a moment before.

He had made it.

There *was* a footnote to the story: two days later the older sister came out on her own. She was determined to walk across the bridge, despite the snipers, despite the Muslims guarding their side of the bridge, who warned her that the Croats would surely kill her and feed her to their dogs. She didn't care, she retorted; she was too old and too tired to live one more day like a rat in a warren. When she reached her sister's, she told her that she *had* heard Jozo, but as her sister had feared, she had thought it was a trick.

Mulling over Jozo's story, I wondered what I would have done. Would I have gone back? Would I have gone over the bridge in the first place? I hoped so, but there was no way of knowing until it happened.

"Jozo," I said as he finished, "I've got to ask: What made you turn around and go back into that bombed-out building when you weren't even sure anyone was there?"

He shrugged and smiled. "It was the right thing to do."

ELEVEN

ROSES

Sarajevo — Driving in from the west, Luke and I caught our first glimpse of Sarajevo around noon, and from a distance, under the dazzling noonday sun, it was quite appealing. But as we approached on the main thoroughfare—a divided highway with a tramline down the middle—we saw how deceiving initial appearances could be. The closer we came to the center of the city, the worse the devastation became, until as we drove along the stretch known as "Sniper Alley," the high-rise office buildings on either side were nothing more than vertical ruins. They looked startlingly like the federal building in Oklahoma City after the bomb tore off its face.

It was a shocking sight, and everywhere we looked we saw more of the same. Passing on our left was the famous Holiday Inn, looking like a giant Rubic's Cube, all of its squares yellow. The most luxurious hotel in Bosnia, it was the only one in the city that was fully functioning. A room cost $180 a night, and only those on generous expense accounts could afford to stay there. During the war, journalists and other old hands always requested a room on the north side, since the south-facing rooms were constantly being shelled. It was here in early April 1992 that the war in

Bosnia had begun. When a spontaneous peace march to protest the possible spillover of the war from Croatia into Bosnia attracted thousands of Sarajevo's citizens, Serb paramilitaries on the high ground of Grbavica had begun firing into the crowd. With those shots the war arrived in Bosnia.

But it was impossible to remain solemn on such a beautiful day as today. It was warm, and the streets were teeming with traffic; even the tram was running. We had one contact in the city: Todd Stoltfus of World Vision, an international humanitarian aid organization that specialized in going into disaster areas—natural or manmade—and helping to rebuild the life that had been there. Todd was their program director for Sarajevo. Arriving at their offices just as he was on his way out to lunch, we joined him.

He looked as though he had stepped out of a relief-workers' recruiting poster. Clean-cut, dressed in a work shirt and jeans, he was medium tall with the sort of broad shoulders that indicated he had once worked with weights. He had natural, wholesome good looks, a quick smile, and a relaxed, easygoing attitude. He seemed, in fact, totally unflappable—exactly the sort of person you would want in charge of multiple construction sites. He asked what we felt like eating, and when we said Bosnian, he took us to his favorite quick lunch place in the old quarter.

On this bright, breezy day in late May, all of Sarajevo seemed to be out taking the air, meeting friends, shopping, or stopping for a coffee or a bite of lunch at one of the outdoor cafés. Everyone was in such a buoyant mood, it was hard to remember that less than a year ago these people had been enduring hell.

Plenty of reminders lay underfoot—so many "roses" left by grenades on the paving stones of the old quarter, there was no point counting them. A rose was Bosnia's irony-tinged name for the circular pattern of scars gouged in the pavement or a sidewalk by the shrapnel of an exploding rocket grenade. Some had come down between buildings so high, I had to marvel at the accuracy of the gunners. Unlike mortars, these grenades fell exactly where the gunners wanted them.

Another grim reminder was the war-wounded; never had I seen so many one-legged men on crutches. I was told that in Mostar eight thousand men had lost one or both legs; undoubtedly there were even more here. And although we did not see any, we knew many children were crippled as well. I tried to remember the last time I had seen a one-legged man on crutches back home. I had seen some after the Vietnam War, but none for many years.

As we entered the old section, the streets narrowed, and we were caught up in a river of pedestrian traffic. The women were so chic, with understated gold jewelry and stunning silk scarves, we might have been in Paris or Rome, except that a number of them favored a dark red, almost burgundy hair coloring that was distinctly Bosnian. There were IFOR officers everywhere, walking in pairs and wearing camouflage battle fatigues. Their distinguishing feature was their different-colored berets. Two tall, thin officers with close-cropped gray hair and pale blue berets turned out to be a two-star general in the French paratroops and his counterpart in the *Legion Etranger*. Two swarthy majors in burgundy berets were Italian *caribinieri*. The two green-beret colonels behind us were American tankers.

Other men and boys wore "camies" as well; they were as in-fashion here as jeans were back home. Whether or not the men wearing them had actually fought in the war, they wanted to give that impression. The real soldiers were easily identified: they were the ones with side arms. During the war, with every paramilitary or militia recruit carrying a Kalashnikov or other automatic weapon, Bosnia had been a bit like the old Wild West. Now only the police and IFOR were allowed to go armed; anyone else caught with a gun would be instantly arrested as a terrorist. But many had not relinquished their weapons; they had merely put them out of sight.

We passed by the open-air marketplace that covered half a city block where dozens of people had been massacred by a surprise grenade. The footage of body parts strewn about and pools of blood everywhere, all faithfully recorded by CNN, probably shocked the world out of its complacency more than any other single photographed event. NATO, responding to world outrage, finally called in air strikes and demanded that the heavy artillery encircling Sarajevo be pulled back. The siege was broken, peace was imposed, and slowly Sarajevo began to wake up. Today, the marketplace was crowded with umbrella-shaded produce carts, each piled high with fresh fruit or vegetables.

When I expressed surprise at how many places were open and flourishing, Todd replied that he, too, was amazed. Not a day went by that another new shop or restaurant didn't open. The resiliency of the Sarajevans was astonishing. At the cafeteria-style restaurant to which he had taken us, we ordered what we wanted by pointing at it, then took a table outside, where we could watch the passing parade. The food, which had names I instantly forgot, tasted much better than it looked.

Before he went back to his office, Todd took us to the national library, or what was left of it. Once it had been an elegant octagonal building of stone, four stories high with an open central interior space and an elaborate skylight. Books containing all the history of Bosnia, including precious volumes several hundred years old, had been stored on shelves that radiated inward from the eight outside walls.

To prove a people never existed, you must first destroy any historical record of their prior existence. A single incendiary grenade had been lobbed though the skylight and exploded on the top floor. Ray Bradbury had informed my generation that books burned at Fahrenheit 451°. The library was soon consumed by a napalm inferno many times that temperature. It quickly burned through the top floor, bringing that raging story down on the third, and soon the second, and then the first. There was no fighting such a fire. In a few hours the heritage of a thousand years lay in a burning heap on the ground floor.

Todd said the building had been pronounced unsafe; there was fear that the eight-sided shell might soon collapse. Standing in the entryway, looking at the fire-blackened walls, and above them at the shattered, twisted frame of the skylight, I noticed that none of the city's birds was here. Strange—they were everywhere else. It was like standing at the entrance of Auschwitz to which no birds came, either. Only this was a crematorium for books.

Why would one people go to such lengths to eradicate the culture of another, I wondered. Even the Nazis, modern history's prize barbarians, had spared Rome. And Hitler's order to burn Paris had been thwarted by one of his own officers. No answer came to me; the depths of Balkan hatred were unfathomable.

As we walked back to Todd's office, he explained the work of World Vision. It was a much larger organization than I had imagined, a consortium of nationalities, spearheaded by the United States, combining the countries' efforts to deliver effective humanitarian aid. World Vision had several relief efforts currently in operation around the globe, and in the past year it had decided to make a major commitment in Bosnia. Wherever it went, its first objective was to determine the greatest need and then how best to go about meeting that need.

I was surprised to learn that the greatest single need in Sarajevo right now was not food or fuel, but *glass*. Of course, the reason was soon obvious: practically every window in the central part of the city—especially those anywhere near the front lines—needed replacing. Literally thousands of new windows were needed, and as Todd spoke I had the thought: *How many bullets had been needed to shatter them all?* Probably a trainload, but they had been available. So great had been Tito's paranoia about Stalin turning on him, that he had amassed a ten-year supply of munitions, which the JNA had maintained. That explained why so many buildings had been gratuitously sprayed with automatic-weapons fire. In most armies, officers and senior noncommissioned officers would abruptly curtail any waste of ammunition. In the hills surrounding Sarajevo, however, men who were physically or psychologically little more than boys had been given heavy-caliber weapons and a virtually unlimited supply of ammo, with no accountability.

World Vision had decided to focus on helping the old and infirm. One by one, they were locating and renovating the war-damaged apartments of couples who were too old, too weak, and too poor to move, let alone help themselves. First they would replace the glass, then they would install insulation, and finally they would refinish the apartment. They had several renovations underway at the same time and were moving as fast as they could before winter set in. If they did not finish enough apartments, the people they were trying to help would literally freeze to death. At 1,800 feet above sea level, Sarajevo was brutally cold in the dead of winter, and fuel was extremely scarce even in peacetime. All the work was done by local workmen under local contractors, whom Todd and his staff hired. In this way World Vision was also helping Sarajevo's economy.

Listening to Todd, I could not remember ever being more proud of an American effort to help the less fortunate in foreign lands. Years ago a few books had painted an extremely unattractive (and widely accepted) portrait of well-intentioned but insensitive and ultimately catastrophic American interventions abroad. World Vision was putting to death the old stereotype image of the ugly American, as it helped Sarajevo emerge from her nightmare, one apartment at a time.

When we got back to Todd's office, his receptionist, Sabina, took us to the apartment of a woman where we could stay for about a sixth of what the Holiday Inn would have cost. It was love at first sight. Our white-haired landlady was at the kitchen window of her third-floor walk-up, leaning out, resting on her forearms. Five small, slightly dented cars were parked below, with just enough room for one more. Laundry was attached by clothespins to a clothesline running from another apartment across the alley by a system of pulleys. In a small patch of shade, a sleeping dog ignored the flies buzzing around him. The scene looked exactly like one Norman Rockwell might have painted half a century ago. This would be our home for the next three days.

Our landlady turned out to be Sabina's great-aunt, and through Sabina she explained that I would sleep in the living room and Luke in her bedroom. Until we left, she would sleep in the kitchen. We were also informed that the city's water was shut off in the evenings from seven to eleven, which accounted for the full bucket of water in the bathroom. The first flush was on the house.

After work the next day, Todd took us in his white jeep on a tour of the city, starting with the site of the 1984 Winter Olympics. This had been Sarajevo's crowning achievement, when the entire world had been impressed by the city's cosmopolitan but fun-loving spirit and charming ways. The winter sports stadium was a shambles now; the entire facility was in ruins, and the area where the speed skating rink had been, where Eric Heiden had won four gold medals, now was converted into an enormous graveyard. The graves were packed so closely together, they were like commuters crowding onto a rush-hour subway, trying to get a few more in.

From there Todd took us to what had been the western front line: a six-foot-deep trench dug literally across the road, deep enough that a man could stand in it and be completely concealed. At one point the trench ran close by the Sarajevo zoo.

"What happened to the animals?" I asked.

Todd hesitated before replying. They'd had a hard time, he said, and he could not talk about it easily. Snipers had waited for anyone foolish enough to try to help the animals. As the animals grew more hungry, they began to cry. People hearing them wanted to help, but the snipers would kill anyone who showed himself. The animals began crying piteously. No one dared help them. And they all starved to death.

We rode on in silence. Just when I thought nothing could elicit deeper revulsion than all I had already seen, I turned a corner and ran into something even more horrific. No one could tell me that Satan didn't exist. Only he could inspire someone to use the pleas of a starving animal to lure the merciful into the sights of his gun.

Todd took us up to Grbavica, the southern heights of Sarajevo where the oppressors were forced by the Dayton

Accord to give back the apartments they had taken. It was the last area of control they had relinquished, and they did so grudgingly, burning and looting as they left, trying to leave it as uninhabitable as possible. Behind them, they had sown mines everywhere. We passed many areas cordoned off with yellow police tape, and those were only the areas in which mines had already been discovered. Such discoveries were usually tragic: not a day went by that Sarajevo did not experience another mine accident, most often set off by children playing.

Atop the hill overlooking the city, next to the old Jewish synagogue and cemetery, both of which had been destroyed in one of the first battles, we stopped and got out, being careful to stay on the pavement. Once this must have been a magnificent view, but now not even the late afternoon sun could soften the total desolation. Immediately below us we saw houses that had all lost their roofs. Farther away stood wrecked office buildings, and farther still, high-rise apartments with all their windows gone. Looking through the window of a sand-bagged bunker, I could make out the Holiday Inn about a mile away. I wondered what it must have been like to sit in this bunker with one of those long, thin-barreled, flat-trajectory guns. From here, you could pull the trigger, punch a hole in that yellow cube, and be completely detached from the ensuing horror at the receiving end.

By sundown we had seen all the destruction we could assimilate; our receptors were on overload. We went down to the old quarter and had supper, asking Todd to fill in the blanks in what we knew of his experience here.

"So, listen," I said, as we ate something wrapped in cabbage leaves, "was the war still going on when you got here?"

Todd laughed. "We'd set up our headquarters in Zenica,

because that city was quiet, while Sarajevo was taking all the hammering. But no sooner do I get there than NATO finally sends in its air strikes and forces the JNA to pull its big guns back. So, you know where they moved them?"

I could guess, but I just waited, smiling.

"Right!" he exclaimed, "Zenica! The day after I got there, they started shelling the downtown area—right at six, when all the office-workers were leaving to go home to supper."

We laughed. "What did you think, when you heard the first one?"

Todd shook his head. "I could not believe how *loud* it was! TV and movies just don't prepare you for the sheer noise of one of those big shells. They rattle windows, they shake buildings—and they shook me!"

I nodded and smiled. "I can remember the first time my parents took me to a fireworks display. I must have been six or seven. It wasn't so bad, until one of those big ones with no visible displays came. It just went *ka-boom* right overhead, and I ran for the car and rolled the windows up."

I tried something that must have been potatoes, and asked, "What's the worst part of your job?"

He thought for a moment. "Having to turn down cases of real need, because there are cases that are even needier." He paused. "And then not having enough money to help all of them, either."

"And the best part?"

He smiled. "That's easy: Seeing the tangible evidence of your work. A newly finished apartment where there had been nothing but a wrecked one before."

I nodded and asked the question I had been saving. "What was the hairiest moment since you got here?"

"That would be the night I and another staffer named

Harry woke up to hear someone trying to steal our car. It was an old Peugeot, and it had a starter problem. So the guy trying to hot-wire it was having trouble getting it started, or we never would have heard him. Harry got this zillion candlepower floodlight, while I searched all over the place for the front-door key. We were on the third floor," he explained and shuddered briefly at the memory. "You know, not finding that key was God saving my life."

He reflected on that, until I said, "Well, then what happened?"

"We went out on the balcony, switched on the floodlight, and yelled at him." He paused. "You'd think he'd hightail it out of there! But this guy was no ordinary car thief. He was bent over the engine with the hood up. Now he straightened up, and he was wearing a skimask. He looked up at us calmly, and then slowly pulled out this huge automatic and aimed it at us. And cocked it."

"C'mon!" I demanded. "What happened?"

"When we heard that little metallic sound, Harry and I both dove for the doorway to get inside. And we stayed inside, until we heard him finally get the car started and drive it away."

We were nonplussed. I remembered Jeff's telling me about the high incidence of car theft up here.

"Was that the end of it?" Luke asked. "Didn't you report it?"

"Sure. And you know what? A few days later the police actually located it, but they didn't pick it up."

"Why not?" I asked.

"Because it was in a mujehadin encampment." I nodded; the mujehadin were mercenaries from Iran, Libya, or Afghanistan. If you were Muslim, they were freedom-fighters; if you weren't, they were terrorists and professional killers.

Todd shook his head. "Not even the police messed with the mujehadin."

"But," I asked, "didn't the Dayton Accord call for all foreign mercenaries to leave the country?"

"Sure, but who's going to make them?" He shook his head. "You know, a lot of people around here regard them as heroes. They're the only ones who came to help when the West was turning a deaf ear on Bosnia's appeals."

After dinner, Todd returned to his office, and we went back to our car. It was not where we had parked it. I was not unduly alarmed; this had happened to me before, usually at Logan Airport in Boston, where I would leave my car on the third level and be sure that I had left it on the fourth. It was probably just around the corner . . . only it wasn't. And then I distinctly remembered parking it by the side of this building, in the midst of several white UNHCR vehicles, all of which were gone now. As was our car, with all my interview tapes and all Luke's camera equipment in the back of it.

Jeff Reed's warning came back to me now, about the high incidence of car theft up north, which Todd had confirmed earlier that day.

Well, it was gone. Now what?

The only thing to do was go back to the World Vision office, and hope that Todd had not already gone home. If he had, we would just have to go to the police. Great. We didn't even know where to find them, let alone how to speak their language. And what could they do, anyway? Take down the license plate and promise to keep an eye out for it? The license plate? We didn't know the license plate.

We walked up the four flights to the World Vision offices and were tremendously glad to see a light under the door. We told Todd what had happened, and he smiled and told us to calm down. "It may not be stolen."

"What?"

"The police may have picked it up, in which case, you can get it back by paying a fine."

"How much?"

"Sometimes it's a lot."

"How much is a lot?"

"Eight hundred Deutschmarks."

That *was* a lot! But it was still preferable to the alternative.

Todd called his second in command, a local woman named Goranka Ivanisevic. She was home and said she would come in. She would take half an hour to get here.

I looked at my watch: it was already 8:30. Should I have Todd tell her not to go to the trouble this late at night? No, we needed all the help we could get.

The next half hour was one of the longest I have ever spent. I paced, and Luke sat. I sat, and Luke paced. Todd worked at his desk, unperturbed.

That night I discovered that while Luke seemed calm, he was as wrung out as I was. I dreaded having to tell Jeff what had happened to his car. And what if it wasn't insured? Did they even have insurance over here? What if we had to replace it? And what about my tapes? If the car was gone, so was the whole first half of this trip. I shrank from having to tell my publisher what had happened. And what were we going to do for transportation? Rent a car and driver?

The door opened; Goranka came in. She was out of breath from the four flights, but she was smiling. "You can relax," she exclaimed. "It's not stolen!"

The police had impounded it. They had picked it up with their spider,[10] and it was in their pound, about a ten-minute

---

[10] The next night, we saw the spider in action. It was a small flatbed truck with a crane that had a long arm with four slings attached to the end of it. One man swung the crane arm over the offending vehicle—in this case, a small, white, UNHCR two-door parked on the sidewalk—while another man put a sling around each of its wheels. The first man raised the arm, swung the sedan over the bed and lowered it, and they drove away. The entire operation took less than four minutes.

walk from here. The fine was fifty marks, and she thought we could get it tonight, if we were willing to pay a tip. We were.

As we walked over, I asked if she was related to the tennis star, Goran Ivanisevic. He was her first cousin, and she had traveled with him on the circuit. When we arrived at the pound, she negotiated the tip for us: another twenty-five marks for them to pay the fine for us at the post office in the morning. I doubted they would ever make it to the post office, but having the car back was worth the extra money. I never did find out what law we had broken. Todd suggested it was simply that our car had Croat plates, and this was a Muslim town. The current Muslim-Croat Federation was a marriage arranged in Dayton; the Muslims may have forgiven the Croats for what had happened down in Mostar, but they had not forgotten.

We thanked Todd and Gora again, and I marveled at how much they had done for us. Never again would I object to having my work interrupted when an out-of-town visitor dropped in unexpectedly. I owed such a debt of hospitality to the Body of Christ that I determined to drop whatever I was doing and give the person my undivided attention. (Of course, this resolution was put to the test as soon as I arrived home, and I had to be reminded of my promise.)

Arriving back at our bed and breakfast, we tucked in our car so that its license plate was in the shadows. Our landlady smiled and nodded from her kitchen window, and it was somehow comforting to know that she had waited up for us.

It had been a long day. We had seen enormous destruction, a terrible residue of hate, and I was grateful that the scene lingering in my mind as I fell asleep went in the opposite direction.

Up on the heights of Grbavica, as we began to come down, I had heard the sound of hammering, which seemed to be coming from directly below. Going over to the guardrail, I peered down and saw a middle-aged man and his wife working. They were on their patio, framing in a new doorsill. At the corner of the patio was a stack of red tiles waiting to replace the ones that had been lost when a hole had been blown in the roof. Replacing them would be a major undertaking, a weekend project that needed the help of friends. In the meantime, they would put in this door while they still had enough daylight to work.

TWELVE

EARNING TRUST

The sun streamed in through the west windows of the small, neat one-room apartment of a tall, thin, angular American in his late thirties. David Lively, like Todd, was single; it seemed to be a prerequisite for missionary duty in Bosnia. He had lived for the first six months of his tour in a UN refugee camp, and the first six weeks of that in a tent. In manner, David was shy and self-effacing, except when it came to encouraging the young converts with whom he was working; then with quiet enthusiasm he would help them to find balance in their daily life. This he did in their own language, carrying on the tradition of all missionaries: live with a people, eat what they eat, respect their ways, learn their language. When you have earned their trust, they might ask you why you have come.

I asked David how the missionary business was doing here.

Sarajevo was fertile ground, he said. Before the war, the capital of Bosnia enjoyed the highest standard of living in any Eastern Bloc country. Perhaps as a consequence, personal faith had not been very high on the average citizen's priority list. Then came the war, which overturned the city's applecart. Now *everyone* was needy. The only trouble was that religion was almost always spoken of in terms of its political implications.

Before the war, no one in Sarajevo had thought of himself or herself as primarily Catholic or Orthodox or Muslim. It was like your driver's license; it was in your wallet somewhere, but you would have to fish in there to get it. Now, your identity was right on your shirtfront, whether you liked it or not. If you were a Muslim, you may not have set foot inside a mosque in years, but now you were a Muslim first, and perhaps you had better start following the observances of Islam—that is, if you knew what was good for you in the new Bosnia.

Many people were genuinely needy now, genuinely searching for spiritual answers, David said, yet they were resistant to being shoehorned into their traditional churches. So a new approach to faith (new to Bosnia) that offered Jesus as the answer to any problem had definite appeal.

David had arranged for me to meet and talk with some of the people with whom he worked. At his request, we spoke in English, so that they could strengthen their use of the language.

Dragan Nedic was short, crew-cut, quiet, and in his midthirties. His father was a Serb, his mother a Croat. In the eyes of some in the new Bosnia for whom such things were important, his lineage would make him Serbian, by extraction. In God's eyes, Dragan said, he was just a Christian, entrusted with the leadership of a small but growing church of mostly young, new Christian converts. He was not their pastor, he explained, because he was not ordained. He was merely their shepherd until such time as God provided a pastor for them.

Another member of that flock was the young woman sitting next to him. This was Sandra, five years younger, happy, quiet, of Catholic parents. They had married four months before. They would have married four years before, but the war had intervened. When it came, Dragan was a student at the University of Sarajevo. He was immediately mobilized and joined the Bosnian army's defense of the city. He had not thought the war would actually happen; none of his friends had. People of the three different ethnic groups had been living together in peace all of his life; there was no reason for them to divide. When it happened, he was shocked and sure that it would all be over in a couple of weeks.

But immediately he had a conflict: how could he take up a gun, when he believed that God did want him to kill anyone? Yet how could he refuse, when it was the law of his country? In the end, he decided to be obedient to the call-up and trust God to keep him from taking another's life.

Army life was another shock to Dragan. All his life he had been an independent spirit, doing pretty much what he wanted to, whenever and however he wanted to do it. That, he discovered, was not the army way. Not only did he have to obey orders, he was expected to act and even think as everyone else did for the duration of the war.

He had little opportunity to share his faith. Most of the men were Muslims, and the moment a person brought up Christ, they thought he must be Orthodox or Catholic, trying to talk to them about his religion. It was a decidedly hostile atmosphere.

So he decided just to live his faith, as best he could, and let his actions speak for themselves. Gradually he made friends in his unit, but that only complicated the tension under which he lived. God said: Thou shalt not kill. But what if they were in a situation in which the lives of his friends depended on his willingness to protect them? What if they were in the front line together, and their platoon was given the order to attack?

Inevitably the thing he feared most came upon him: his platoon was sent forward to launch a surprise attack on a well-defended Serb position. He seemed doomed; many people were going to be killed, and he was about to be called upon to do his share of the killing.

Crawling forward on their hands and knees through heavy underbrush, they came within fifteen yards of the houses and trenches that comprised the enemy position. From their line of concealment, Dragan and his friends could actually see the faces and hear the voices of the men they soon would be assaulting. The enemy far outnumbered them, but Dragan's platoon would have the advantage of surprise.

Any moment now, the order to attack would come. Dragan grew desperate. "God, I don't want to kill anybody! But there's nothing I can do now; You'll have to help."

And so they waited, every muscle tensed, ready to explode into action—charging, shooting, throwing hand grenades. A few yards away, the enemy went about their routine—bored, passing time, cracking jokes.

They went on waiting for half an hour, an hour. Dragan's platoon relaxed, but only a little; they knew that at any moment the signal would be given. They waited a second hour and a third. Combat in Bosnia was no different than anywhere else: hours of sheer boredom punctuated by moments of stark terror.

After four full hours, someone in Dragan's platoon got careless. Four hours was an interminable length of time to lie motionless; maybe he had to—

They were seen! Shouts of alarm went up along the

enemy lines, and machine gun, mortar, cannon, and small-arms fire poured into their position. They were too close to get up and run, too close even to stick up their heads enough to fire back. All they could do was hug the earth and hope for relief.

Dragan watched in horror as bullets kicked up dirt in front of him, beside him. No bullets hit him, though several of his friends were killed, and others were wounded. For three hours they endured this ordeal, until finally darkness fell and they could crawl out, one by one.

That was the closest he had come to killing anyone, and he had come a lot closer to being killed himself. He had not thought of that episode for a long time and did not like thinking of it now.

Ruja, twenty-two years old, was petite, dark-haired, dark-eyed, bright, and effervescent. She was studying English in college, hoping one day to use it professionally. David Lively encouraged her to take her new language out for a spin, and she did fine.

Before the war, Ruja's family was culturally Muslim, but in reality nonreligious. Her own spiritual interest extended about as far as astrology, and even that only occasionally. Then, just before the war began, some young people she knew told her about Jesus, and she became a Christian. She kept putting off telling her parents, not at all sure how they would take it, and then the war broke out.

Her father went off to fight in the war, leaving her and her mother at home. As in Mostar, the relentless, hammering bombardment took its toll on everyone's nerves. Some came close to cracking under the strain, and her mother was one.

Ruja helped her as much as she could, even reading the Bible to her, which seemed to calm her.

As for herself, she had been badly frightened when the grenades landed close to their home for the first time. But she felt God would keep her from getting hurt. There was no church for her at that time; with all the snipers and shelling, it was impossible for Christians to meet. Nonetheless, Ruja used the time to get to know God better. She prayed every day and read her Bible almost every day, though the "falcons" (as she called her various distractions and interruptions) tried to take her away from her reading.

Meanwhile, though her parents were still not religious, they were becoming more and more Muslim in their outlook. Before the war they had never paid any attention to a person's nationality. Now they did, which made it all the harder for Ruja to tell them what had happened to her.

Finally she summoned the nerve to tell her mother. But her father was another matter. Since she knew she had to do it, she stopped putting it off and told him.

Her father said little; it was not easy for him to express feelings.

Her mother said, "I don't understand this Christianity, but I understand you. I have seen you in many hard times, many difficult situations; everything you have done is good. So I trust you. If this Christianity is helping you to be the way you are, then you may continue to do it."

Ruja tried to explain her faith to her mother, but it was too hard. So she asked God to show her the way, when it was time. As for her father, when he came home wounded, all she could do was thank God for saving his life. She had no hate in her heart for those who had fired the grenade, nor for anyone involved in the war. All she could do was thank God for his life, and she sensed that somehow this would be the thing that God would use to reach her father.

After the war was over, her church started up again, and with her parents' blessing Ruja began attending.

Then her aunt and uncle got wind of what she was doing. They were furious. Her aunt came over to talk to her mother, sister to sister; she said that Ruja had fallen into the clutches of a sect and said many other terrible things about her.

Her mother, showing a great deal of courage, stood up for Ruja. But Ruja's newfound faith put a tremendous strain on her parents, especially on their relationships with the Muslim community in which they lived. In spite of external pressure, her parents continued to allow her to go to church. They liked what they saw happening in her, and they trusted her.

"I believe in God's Word," Ruja told me, patting her Bible. "He said that the families of believers would believe" (Acts 16:31). She shrugged and smiled. "I'm a believer. I think one day my family will be, too."

THIRTEEN

EASTER PEOPLE

Sarajevo — One afternoon about halfway through the trip, we had an incredible three hours when we had nothing scheduled. Luke went off to take pictures, and I drifted. In our contemporary world of compressed time, drifting is a lost art. You start walking, with no plan or purpose. You just walk, letting whim or circumstance be the guide.

That balmy afternoon I walked by an auto repair garage that was so small it barely had room for one car. And because one car was inside, and another needed immediate attention, the mechanic was out in the street, on his back underneath it.

I walked by a bakery, whose smell reminded me that my favorite Bosnian food is the bread they bake. It was thick, chewy, and flavorful, and it went a long way toward stretching a thin soup.

I passed the bridge over the Miljacka River, where Archduke Ferdinand had been assassinated eighty-two summers before. That act precipitated World War I and so much of the Balkan upheaval that followed. A little war was being waged there now, on the sidewalk in front of the bridge: a little dog on a leash and a little boy were having a tug-of-war, and the dog was winning.

In the old section of the city I stopped at an outdoor café for a coffee. The waiter arrived with a little silver tray holding a small, squat silver pot with a long thin handle, a very small silver bowl with brown sugar in it, and an even smaller silver cup, about half the size of a demitasse. While the five-century reign of the Ottoman Turks in the Balkans was universally abhorred, one custom the Turks left behind was universally appreciated: their coffee. With great ceremony it was served wherever we went in Bosnia—a highly valued ritual of hospitality which would have been uncommonly gauche to refuse.

The waiter asked if I would like him to pour me a cup, and I nodded. He did and bowed and departed. With a small silver spoon I added some sugar, stirred, and took a sip—and tried not to frown. It was an acrid, turgid brew with a bitter aftertaste. You had to be careful to leave the last sip in the cup, as there was a great deal of sediment in Turkish coffee. Above all, it was strong, just the thing to jumpstart a cold engine block: a jolt from a *quatre-tasse*.

I savored the coffee and the free time, and thought about all that we had seen and experienced so far, and what I would remember of it. For all the devastation, for all the crippled warriors and young trauma cases and grief-stricken widows, the thing that bothered me right now were the animals in the this city's zoo, left to starve slowly to death in their cages. I didn't know why it troubled me so much. It was never a good idea to ask God to show you what He wanted you to see, I thought dourly, because He usually showed you more than you bargained for. And the effect usually went deeper than you intended.

Part of my reaction to the animals, I was now seeing, came from long-buried guilt. I had not always been an animal lover. As a child, cruelty, sudden violence, and indifference to their pain all seemed viable options where animals were concerned. As I grew older, my father taught me to respect all animals, even the ones we hunted. He had one dictum: Never shoot anything you are not going to eat. I could still hear the shotgun pellets plinking onto the butter plates as we ate the pheasant we had shot. But when I was a boy with my own .22, I did not always follow that dictum. I was a good shot and killed many small animals at great range. One day I shot a robin; when I came closer to inspect my shot, I found she had three babies in her nest. They would all starve to death now because of what I had done. I stopped killing after that.

But in my imagination I did not stop. The aftermath of this war was showing me that a lot more murder resided in my own heart than I wanted to admit.

It came out in ways that surprised me. A well-crafted revenge movie could bring it forth. The hero, a normal likable guy (like me), was suddenly and violently abused by an evildoer, who did horrible things to the hero and the ones he loved. Frustrated rage and fear welled within our hero (me), until finally at the end of the movie, it was payback time: the situation was reversed, and the victim had the upper hand. "Kill him!" I would find myself muttering at the screen, *"Kill him!"*

And what about all the time I spent fantasizing revenge? When I perceived that I had been sorely mistreated or wrongfully judged in some situation over which I had no control, in my mind I would rewrite the script, and then replay the scene several times, sometimes on an endless loop. Then I would imagine the next encounter, and this time I would have the best lines or the weight of evidence on my side. I repeatedly imagined appealing my case to a higher authority who would see the injustice that had been done and would set matters right, forthwith. And I would be able to witness the perpetrator's getting what he or she so richly deserved.

That was the one drawback to God's saying that vengeance was His: you never got to watch it. You couldn't even be sure He would do it in this lifetime. (For some evil-doers, eternal damnation wasn't enough, I thought then.)

I took another sip and remembered the last time I had had a cup of Turkish coffee. It had been two days before, down in Mostar with Sister Janja. Now she was someone who understood the meaning of forgiveness!

I smiled to recall her—her black hair tinged with gray, the eyes a little sadder, though they still sparkled when she teased. I had met her on my first trip to Medjugorje and had come to know her on subsequent visits. I got to know her even better during the war, when she was the superior of the Mostar convent. During the bombardment, her phone seemed to be the only working line in Hercegovina. It was an old post-office model, put in service in the 1930s and given to the convent when the post office upgraded its equipment. (In Bosnia, if you did not own a phone, the only place from which to make a long-distance call was one of the booths at the post office.) It had a long cord, so that she could take it down to the basement when the shells were falling. She called it her miracle phone—and I had to admit, I never failed to get a 3:00 A.M. call through to her. Then I would type up her news, fax it to Jeff in Dallas and Mike Einarsen in Chicago and Mimi Kelly in New Orleans and Sister Isabel in Steubenville, Ohio, and they would put it on the network.

As Easter of 1992 approached, the bombardment intensified. When I expressed concern for her safety, she laughed. "Don't worry; we will survive. We are Easter people, and our song is Alleluia!"

After six weeks of incessant shelling, however, she had lost her resiliency; they all had. They were just enduring. One morning, the shelling was so close I could hear the detonations through the receiver. She told me that the house across the street from them had just been demolished. She sounded very weak.

How long had it been since she had eaten?

Four days.

How long since she had slept?

She couldn't remember.

Listening to her, I suddenly realized that she might not live through this, that this might, in fact, be our last conversation. She must have had a similar premonition. When I asked her if I could pray for anything specific, she said, "Please pray that if now is our time, that we go to God with only love in our hearts for those who are doing this, because sometimes that is hard."

But she didn't die. Though their convent received a direct hit the next day, it was not an incendiary shell; it only put a big hole in the roof. After the dust settled, she smiled and said, "Sisters, first we will have our morning coffee, and then we will clean up the mess."

Later on during the war, Sister Janja and Father Svet were flown to New York for a major humanitarian relief effort. There was a black-tie dinner, and they were seated at one of the head tables. Next to Sister Janja was Peter Jennings. She looked him in the eye and challenged him: "You are a journalist. You should come over to Bosnia yourself and see what is happening there." So he did. For a week, ABC's evening news originated from Mostar and Sarajevo— and that week probably did more than anything else to raise America's consciousness of what was really happening in Bosnia.

I added Sister Janja to my growing list of peacemakers.

In the sidewalk in front of me was a grenade rose. I wondered if anyone had been where I was now when it had landed and how many it might have killed. My mind started going down the path of hating the war-makers again, but I brought it back.

Payback time—the Balkan darkness of unforgiveness was mine, too. In fact, it was my core sin. Not pride or lust or jealousy, or even egomania. Unforgiveness. I seemed to have 20/20 recall of wrongs that had been done to me, even years after the fact. I remembered them in meticulous detail, in all their layers of truth and shadings of meaning. As my wife put it, I got "cased" on people. She was right: I would keep case files, and the files were always open for fresh evidence or documentation.

I, of course, put it less unflatteringly: I would simply say that I would like to shut certain people out of my life, like turning off the spigot of their personality and never turning it on again. To me, they would cease to exist. But obviously life doesn't work that way; often you wind up having contact with that person frequently, sometimes every day.

Unforgiveness like mine—fantasizing about payback time, about God's vengeance—was sick. No one knew what caused cancer, and certainly none of my doctors had had a clue about what had brought on mine. But my wife suspected a spiritual connection might exist between it and all the hurts I had chosen to harbor.

Nikola Skrinjaric's church had held a reconciliation service. Some Lutherans had come down from Germany, and they had asked the congregation to forgive them for what their countrymen had done to Yugoslavia during World War II. One had responded, "We forgive. But we do not forget." Yet how could there be real forgiveness, said a friend of

Nikola's, without forgetting? How indeed? Like any good Christian, I had forgiven those who had trespassed against me. But had I really? Then why did I still remember?

And I recalled the words of Henri Nouwen in *The Road to Daybreak*: "By not forgiving, I chain myself to a desire to get even, thereby losing my freedom."

All at once it struck me: in His prayer, God says that He forgives us *as* we forgive others. I certainly wanted Him to forget the things for which I had asked Him to forgive me. But the nature of His forgiveness was predicated on my own. It was time to start forgetting.

If I learned nothing else from Bosnia and her tormented bondage to payback time, that insight was worth the trip.

FOURTEEN

THE WHITE SEA

A field of white markers passed by on our left, as the road wound north out of Sarajevo. It was a graveyard, one of the new ones dug to handle the overflow of dead from the siege that had recently ended. These emergency graveyards were everywhere: on soccer pitches or in parks or in farmer's fields like this one. Under the morning sun the wooden shafts marking the graves (not crosses, for the majority of the occupants were Muslim) made a gleaming sea of white, in stark contrast to the bright green of the newly scythed grass. But this sea had more markers than the field could contain; it washed up the side of the adjacent hill to the tree line, where three open graves awaited occupants.

The white sea was receding in my rearview mirror when we passed a house with slabs of marble of all sizes and shadings in front of it. Presumably a local laborer had taken up carving headstones. With Bosnia's economy in a shambles, people did whatever they could to bring in some money. People wanted proper gravestones. If you were good with your hands and could use a chisel, you provided them. A hundred yards further along we encountered another front yard with slabs of marble. Memorializing grief had become a cottage-industry in Sarajevo.

The field of white markers reminded me of Arlington or Gettysburg, but it was different. In those graves lay soldiers who had accepted the possibility of their death as part of the battle they were fighting. The new graveyards of Bosnia contained mostly women and children or men too old to fight. This war had been waged against noncombatants. A sense of peace pervades Arlington and other such gardens of stone—a tranquillity over the resting place of men and women who had given their lives in an honorable cause. This sea of white knew no such peace.

In Mostar and now Sarajevo, we had seen too many graveyards, too much devastation. We had lost our capacity to react, as each site or harrowing tale deserved. The people who survived wanted us to see what had been done to them, so that we could tell others. At first we made an effort to find fresh words to express the revulsion that each new item or incident evoked. But after a while we just numbly shook our heads and chronicled the story and moved on.

But this morning was gorgeous. We had the windows open, and the air had the clean, fresh smell of late blooms and tilled earth. A typical farm here was small by American standards—not more than ten or twelve acres. The family might have a cow and a few chickens, maybe a tractor and some other mechanical equipment. They even might have a car, as well as a truck. But the farm would have been in the family for several generations, with each generation striving to improve it a little or add to it.

When the sun was shining, Bosnia was breathtaking. And in the distance, as everywhere, were the mountains—so old they were rounded and chalky gray, and so windswept they were often bare, save for a few gnarled, close-to-the-ground firs. On all but the steepest slopes, small houses clung to the sides. Father Svet, who was born in such a house and grew up among the mountain people, said that the mountains were within them. They were like parents; they didn't give much, but their children didn't need much. And they were always there.

Because of the absence of lumber, the modest houses we were passing were mostly made from blocks of red clay, faced without and within with white stucco. Their red-tiled roofs were pitched steeply to shed snow; from a distance they looked like clusters of alpine chalets. But their charm evaporated as one drew nigh. Every last house had been rendered uninhabitable—gutted by fire or with a gaping shell-hole, the doors gone and windows shot out. In village after village, the destruction was thorough and systematic; not a single home had been spared. It would be a long time before anyone ever lived there again.

Driving along on such a beautiful day, we had difficulty imagining what it must have been like here during the war. We Americans had never had a conqueror roll over our land, never been utterly at another's mercy, subject to his slightest whim. We had never cried out to friends abroad, only gradually to realize that they would do nothing to help us. Historically one region of America, the South, did have an implanted memory of what this war was like; Sherman's march to the sea, as he burned everything in front of him and left nothing standing or edible behind him, was similar. But the Union general's swath was only fifty miles wide; fully two-thirds of Bosnia had been laid waste.

"Watch it!" warned Luke, and I braked hard for a hay cart creeping along, whose heaped-high load took up three-quarters of the road. It was pulled by a two-wheeled mini-tractor that looked like a big roto-tiller. We had seen several of those little pullers, as well as the traditional dray horses, which were slower but needed no gas.

It took a while to get back up to speed. We were traveling as fast as conditions allowed, which was about 80 kilometers, not miles, per hour though it felt like the latter. One simply could not drive faster—and this was one of the best roads in the country.

Spanning the highway ahead of us was the graceful arch of a free-form concrete bridge. In its center sat a squat, dark-brown vehicle looking like an armored toad. On the side facing us, in large white capitals were the initials "IFOR." A soldier in a burgundy beret and camouflage uniform stood beside the vehicle, cradling an automatic weapon and observing our approach. Another sat in the vehicle's open top hatch, equally bored. I knew from being in the navy how time crawled when you were standing a four-hour watch with nothing to do.

I speculated that their sole purpose was to be seen by anyone coming or going on the main road to Zenica. We had seen many such vehicles during our stay; indeed, if you were jaywalking (or in Sarajevo, jayrunning) and did not quite make it, there was a fair chance the vehicle that hit you would have IFOR on it. As if by confirmation, a few minutes later a convoy of dark brown vehicles swept past us going in the opposite direction—half a dozen troop carriers, led by two "Humvee's," the 1990s equivalent of the utilitarian jeep. This modern version, with a variety of antennae for mobile communication, was much bigger and brawnier than the ordinary jeep, with a wider stance and a higher undercarriage. It looked like a water spider on steroids. Bringing up the rear of the column was a heavier model with a massive fifty-caliber machine gun mounted on it. The expressions of the drivers and others visible were deadly serious.

All in all, it was an impressive display, as it was meant to be. We had seen many such convoys; you could not spend a day on the road in Bosnia, any road, without seeing several. They were always on the move and always looking immensely purposeful. After a while it dawned on me that these high-speed maneuvers were the modern equivalent of gunboat diplomacy. In the previous century ambassadors found that a very persuasive technique for dealing with an intransigent or belligerent warlord was to station just off-shore some very large boats with very large guns, flying the flag of the ambassador's country, so that the warlord could look out the window and see them.

The predecessors of the IFOR vehicles now roaming Bosnia had been white, lightly armored cars with the blue initials UN on their sides. These United Nations Protection Force (UNPROFOR) vehicles were universally despised; they were neither forceful, nor could they provide protec-tion. The UN had been operating under an impossible man-date: to resist through negotiation but not coercion the eth-nic cleansing by those who were using a great deal of force.

IFOR was indeed a horse of a different color: they had already demonstrated their willingness to use force, and they were under orders to pursue aggressively anyone who dared confront them. And therefore nobody did. These convoys, and the massive, heavily armored, long-barreled tanks that intimidated approaching traffic at the IFOR checkpoints in the Serb corridor, were just a reminder, but an effective one: not a single hostile challenge had occurred since IFOR had arrived.

But what would happen when IFOR left? President Clinton had promised the American people that he would bring the troops home one year after he deployed them as our share of the NATO commitment. He might break such a promise, but not in an election year. If the United States did pull out, would the rest of NATO remain? Not likely; they had been none too keen on coming in the first place. Everyone we had spoken to in Bosnia believed (or fervently hoped) that the United States would leave at least a token force. They had done as much in Germany and Korea. "Give peace a chance" went the old saying. But one year was not much of a chance; from what we had seen, more like fifteen or twenty were necessary.

If IFOR did leave, it would be worse than anything that had gone on before. Because the world, in effect, would have washed its hands of Bosnia. That would be the signal to the bully that he again could have free rein of the schoolyard. The hatred would burn and burn. And some geopolitical experts privately, cynically, advised that it might be for the best: like a fire in a trash dump, just let it burn until it burned itself out.

The first thing to die would be hope. And in its place would come fear. (Heaven help those who had sided with the peacemakers.) Fear was the instrument of control for totalitarian states. The Communists were masters at controlling through fear; when East Germany gained its freedom in 1989, the world learned that their secret police had kept dossiers on fully one-third of the entire population. One had difficulty comprehending such a statistic.

But a friend of mine, Bill Basansky, brought it home for me some years ago. He had grown up in the Ukraine under the Communists and had escaped with his family. When I met him, he had been in America for more than twenty years and was a professor of Russian at a major university. One day the Russian ambassador visited the campus, accompanied by two KGB agents. When Professor Basansky met the gaze of one of them, he could not look away. Unable to breathe, he was suddenly trembling; it was as if all the intervening years, all the freedom and security he had enjoyed in the United States, had melted away. He was back in Ukraine at their mercy. And as he stared into the agent's eyes, he knew the KGB man was aware of what he was feeling. And in order that he would know it for certain, the KGB man slightly nodded at him. For several days afterward he could not shake the sense of cold dread that gripped him. And he was a man of prayer.

Some Americans *did* have a racial memory of the experience of living under that kind of fear: the descendants of three million slaves. But for most of us, that kind of fear—the kind you lived and ate and lay down and slept with—was unimaginable. The people of Bosnia had just been through a war whose ferocity had been unequaled since World War II. In that previous war, however, soldiers had fought soldiers; civilians were left out of the actual combat. It was true that the entire Jewish civilian population and many others were systematically shipped off to concentration camps, where six million perished. But such extermination was done out of sight, with a great deal of care to hide it from the world. In this war, instead of going to all that trouble, the soldiers had simply killed the civilians where they found them—in their homes and cities. And so the fear—that it was not really over, that it would soon start up again—lay like a poisonous pool in a fetid jungle, consuming any hope that might drop into it.

Yet hope did exist in Bosnia, even in the midst of the growing despair. One had to poke among the ashes to find it, but it was there, like green shoots emerging from scorched earth.

I eased up on the accelerator. Up ahead were two policemen standing by a small green patrol car in a pull-off. The younger officer held out a yellow paddle with the word "STOP" on it and waved us over.

I figured the trouble was probably our Croatian license plate. It was enough to bring out any number of paddles— what old Bosnian hands called "lollipops." Producing the car's registration and our passports, I smiled and said, "American journalists." He did not smile back as he handed the registration and passports to his partner. They kept them long enough for me to have the faintest taste of fear. In the States when the police pulled me over, I usually deserved it. The experience was unpleasant but not fear-provoking. But we weren't in the States now.

When the officer finally came back with our papers, Luke and I had adopted a serious demeanor and refrained from idle chatter. Still unsmiling, he returned our papers and nodded us on our way.

FIFTEEN

One Village at a Time

Zenica — We had an hour before we were due to meet Chalon Lee, World Vision's head of operations in all Bosnia. While Luke reviewed his latest batch of videos, I strolled the terraces of the Dom Penzionera where we were staying. In back were long strips of vegetable garden, about twenty plots maybe twenty feet by a hundred feet, probably rented to neighbors, with corn, peas, tomatoes, and onions coming up. The *next* time there was a food shortage in this industrial city, at least some of the citizenry would be ready.

The view in front was of distant hills with grazing meadows and topped by copses of trees. These not-quite-mountains were beautiful—hazy green with soft golden overtones from the setting sun. On the one to the left a few cows were slowly making their way back to the barn. Little wisps of cottonwood blossoms drifted on the afternoon breeze, completing the magic.

All at once, I was overwhelmed with love for Bosnia, the whole crazy, tormented, patchwork quilt of a country. I loved the people, all of them, and especially the quiet heroes we had been meeting—the ones who instinctively did the right thing under extreme pressure, who daily risked their lives for others and thought nothing of it, who gave away all their food without thinking about it. Who stayed calm, when maniacs waving guns were screaming at them. Who ran into burning buildings to save old nuns, or outran a barrage to try to find a scared old woman. I loved them all, and I wanted to be like them.

The Bosna River was broad and shallow as it passed by Zenica, and in the last light of day, a fisherman in a bikini, who had apparently been working on his tan earlier in the afternoon, stood a few feet into the river, making casts with a long fly rod. He was taking his time, running his line out, and back, and further out, letting the fly alight on a calm part of the river's bend. He would wait a moment, then jig the line ever so slightly, drawing it back in, an arm-length at a time. He was good; in fact, were it not for his bizarre apparel, he might have been on the Gallatin River outside of Bozeman.

I felt immensely peaceful sitting on the tree-shaded balcony of a restaurant, overlooking him and that river, with the drooping trees at the water's edge. In the distance the sun limned the rims of the hazy mountain/hills. We all sat in silence for a moment, recollecting ourselves. Chalon Lee had been joined by an Australian named Judy, who was down from their office in Tuzla for a meeting they were attending later.

Thin, blond, single, and focused, Chalon spoke with a trace of a Georgia accent, but after ten years in the field, it was pretty well gone. She had seen service in Chad, Mali, and Rwanda before coming here; this was actually her fifth conflict zone, though she assured us that each war had its own personality.

In assessing the reconstruction needs of postwar Bosnia, her organization had a multidisciplinary strategy. The first need was physical reconstruction: Bosnia had two million displaced people, who, where possible, needed to be returned to their homes, if they were ever going to feel any peace or hope for the future and if there were ever to be any meaningful reconciliation. At the same time, the other needs of their communities had to be met: schools, social infrastructure, clinics, as well as an economic recovery initiative.

They made loans to small businesses and religious groups, to get the local economy going. For example, most recently they had launched a mushroom farm, a juice factory, and a car repair shop. With 70 percent unemployment and 300,000 recently demobilized soldiers, jump-starting the economy had the highest priority. A soldier who could not provide for his family was going to be increasingly discontented, which obviously would inhibit the peace-building process. Anything that would help reintegrate these people into the civilian sector was worthwhile. And because the free-enterprise system was relatively new, they had to train people in business, as well as make loans and monitor them. They also had to set up indigenous financial institutions, so that eventually the people could make their own loans. The whole objective was to make the Bosnians self-sufficient as quickly as possible.

World Vision also dealt with the whole psychosocial aspect, which involved treatment of trauma, conflict resolution, grief resolution, stress management, and other related activities. Here again, they were training qualified Bosnian personnel increasingly to take over these responsibilities themselves.

I shook my head; the whole undertaking was mind-boggling. As operations director, Chalon was overseeing different program components and making sure a coherent strategy existed for enhancing the impact for the beneficiaries. That meant ensuring that the operations were well carried out and that they stayed on schedule.

They had just begun to reconstruct an entire village: Makjenovac, south of Doboj, about an hour and a half north of Zenica. As the village had been squarely on the front line, it had taken a pounding from both sides. The people had fled, of course; the first time Chalon went there, the place was a ghost village—completely abandoned, the homes gutted, roofs down, doors and windows blown out.

But the villagers had not fled far, just into the neighboring area. Although their homes were destroyed, they were ready, willing, and anxious to move back. World Vision was in the process of revitalizing that community by rebuilding seventy homes: reconstructing the roofs, weatherizing the houses, and installing wood and coal stoves, and providing tools for food production. They also had been assessing the school needs; in reviving a community, a functioning school for the children is absolutely essential. A school is more than proof of enduring stability; in a way, it is the future.

I knew what she meant. I told Chalon that earlier that afternoon we had visited a new high school, where 486 students—Serbs, Muslims, and Croats—were learning and playing together. Their principal hoped that their school would be a new model for Bosnia.

Chalon nodded. The villagers she had been describing were determined to go back as soon as possible, even though the area was laced with mines and booby traps and the month before, four people had been killed by a mine. Each time Chalon returned, more people were back working on their homes. After having recruited former soldiers to help them get rid of the mines, they were there, sweeping out debris and planting their gardens. Despite all they had been through, they still had enough hope and energy to try to rebuild their lives.

The political assessments and commentaries that crossed Chalon's desk, however, were becoming more and more morbid; they were even talking of institutionalizing the partitioning of the country, in the event that the federation collapsed. Chalon smiled sadly. In their line of work, they had to be realists: Bosnia's problems were not over. When IFOR left, fighting might well break out again. The hope was that with the sides now more balanced, one side would not be so vulnerable to the others and the balance of power would prevent a large outbreak. A renewal of conflict on a broad scale would be "very disappointing."

"And yet," I said, intrigued, "you look optimistic. Why?"

"When you go out into the villages, you see small things that are happening—elements of humanity that can endure, can overcome," she said, becoming enthusiastic, in spite of the long day she had put in. "These people don't care about political parties. They don't have military ambitions. They just want to garden, have a home, be normal citizens. They want a settled life, to go back to work on their farms, to be able to have coffee with their friends."

We looked at the river. The shadows were all the way across it now, and it had grown too cold for the fly fisherman.

"It's a real privilege to be here," Chalon abruptly said. "The people who give financially—they contribute just as much, but they don't have the blessing of actually seeing it happen. It's sort of like they're one step away."

The mountain peaks in the distance were still glowing in the sun. "You said this was your fifth conflict zone. How is this one different from the others?"

She laughed. "I've gotten pretty good at spotting mines. The other day I happened to notice an anti-tank mine buried in the soft dirt of a gully beside the road."

"What did you do?"

"I showed it to an IFOR soldier, who thanked me and had a demining crew come and remove it." She shook her head. "Listen, you guys, if you ever get lost," she warned us with a smile as she got up to leave, "and go up the wrong road and have to turn around, just be sure you stay on the pavement!"

Watching her depart, I added her to the list of quiet heroes, this woman intent on rebuilding Bosnia, one village at a time.

SIXTEEN

THE TWENTY-FIFTH OF MAY

Tuzla — By an unplanned coincidence, we arrived in Tuzla on the most important day in the city's postwar experience. And now we stood with the mayor's party waiting at the east end of the Tuzla cemetery, watching the events at the other end. Soon we would join the long, slow procession to the special site where the seventy-one were buried. From where we stood, we could not see the granite memorial or hear the speeches, but we *could* see that the sad and solemn expressions of the passing dignitaries were mirrored in the faces of thousands of onlookers who had gathered.

A flight of small birds winged overhead against a blue sky accented with a few cirrus brushstrokes. It was a warm but not humid late afternoon with a light breeze making being outside delightful—exactly as it had been a year ago.

On this day last year, the war was still on. But it was winding down, and the focus was on Sarajevo where the aggressors had finally provoked the UN into calling down air strikes on their heavy artillery. The guns surrounding Tuzla were silent, and people there sensed that the aggressors were preparing to pull out. They were in a mood to celebrate; they had been cooped up for weeks, first by the shelling, which kept them in their basements, then by endless days of rain, which kept them in their apartments. But on May 25, the sun was finally out.

And so were the people. They strolled and visited, catching up on friends' news, seeing what was in the shops. A festive mood had been present that afternoon, and it kept building. As the shadows lengthened, the streets of the old section in the center of town were thronged with people, young and old. Going for a walk in the early evening had been an urban tradition in Europe for centuries; Tuzla was making up for lost time.

By seven, many of the older ones had gone home for supper, but the teenagers were in no mood for that. After all, didn't May 25 used to be Youth Day, under the old Communist regime? Besides, this was the first chance they'd had to hang out together in ages.

A little after eight, people were surprised to hear a rocket grenade go off. It had been so long since they had heard one, but the past three years had made them experts at assessing proximity and potential danger. This one was too far away to be concerned about.

As twilight gathered, hundreds of people circled the old blocks, just like old times. And where five streets came together forming a little plaza, more than a thousand people mingled. Their sneakers and loafers and smart high-heeled fashion shoes walked over a rose pattern in the asphalt gouged by a grenade that had fallen there the year before. The gunners' artillery maps with grid coordinates had enabled them to place that grenade precisely here, where the most townspeople would be likely to congregate on a warm, late-spring evening. The year before, the shelling had been fairly constant, and a wary citizenry had stayed indoors, out of harm's way. This night was different: the American F-16s were finally airborne; the whole war soon would be over. Things would be back to normal, only better.

At four minutes before nine, the air was rent with the scream of an incoming rocket grenade. People looked up, horrified. They had no time to run, no room to take cover or hit the ground. The last thing they saw was each other's eyes wide with fright, their mouths gaping in horror.

The grenade exploded with a deafening blast. Shrapnel tore through people in all directions. Bodies were ripped open; blood drenched the walls of the surrounding buildings. Severed limbs were strewn everywhere.

For a moment, only the explosion's echo could be heard as it reverberated out from the heart of the city. Then came the groans, and soon the night was filled with the cries of the wounded and dying and the screams of those who loved them.

The little plaza had been transformed into a nightmare of carnage. Mangled bodies of children lay two and three deep in places, like bloody litter. (Of the seventy-one who were massacred that night, sixty-five were children. Two hundred more were wounded.) Those still alive wailed hysterically or sat rocking in numb grief. Some, dazed, staggered down the side streets or wandered in circles. Those who rushed to help were overwhelmed by the sight that confronted them. The entire city went into shock.

It had taken them a full year to recover from this massacre. This afternoon's commemoration would help bring the grieving process to closure, but for some it would never be completed.

It was our group's turn to join the procession. We followed

Dr. Melvida Vlajic, the mayor's deputy for international relations who had invited us to join her party as they went to lay their bouquet at the foot of the memorial. In a group ahead of us were the local Franciscan priest, the local mufti, and the local Orthodox priest. Arriving only a month before,[11] the Orthodox priest had been stunned when the mayor had related to him the details of the massacre. "It is not human beings who did that," he had said, "not people who believed in God." The shared tragedy had united the leaders of the three faiths.

As we slowly processed along the graveled pathway, it occurred to me that this was another one of those automatic-pilot times. Every so often on this trip, I'd had the distinct impression that events were totally out of our hands. Not until we heeded last-minute advice to abandon going to Banja Luka[12] did we know for certain that we would be here on May 25, and even then, we saw no particular significance to that date.

So great had been the impact on the city that instead of burying the dead children with their families or succumbing to the nationalist pressure of some to separate them ethnically, the city had decided that they should all be buried together on the side of a hill with a special memorial. They had been friends in life; let them be friends in eternal rest. That was the desire of the heart of Tuzla, and it was to their memorial that we were going now.

Those who had already laid their wreaths and visited the graves were coming down beside the steps that we were now going up. Among them was an ensemble of youthful folk-dancers in traditional garb. They had performed a dance at

---

[11] When the war began, all Orthodox priests had left for Belgrade.

[12] A Bosnian Serb stronghold, where Croat license plates would have been an invitation to trouble.

the memorial, and now their eyes were streaming tears as they helped one another down the hill. One of our party whispered to me that two of the dead children had been in that troupe.

As we came into view of the hillside graves, we saw hundreds of mourners circulating among them. Parents and other family members were sitting on little benches beside the graves, receiving the condolences of their friends. All of the graves were strewn with bouquets, and most had photographs of the deceased affixed to the headstones. Everywhere one heard the sound of weeping and lamentation. After watching Dr. Vlajic lay her bouquet, our party made its way down from the hillside.

We walked along in silence, each in our thoughts. I was remembering the grief of the mayor, from whom we had learned the details of the tragedy. Selim Beslagic was a cultural Muslim, a middle-aged, crew-cut man with black-rimmed glasses. Before being elected mayor in 1991, he had been a chemical engineer at the big chemical plant that had been one of Tuzla's main industries. He was confident and dynamic, his vigor belying his gray hair. We had requested the interview, having been informed that of all the politicians in Bosnia, he was one of those most in favor of returning to the old multicultural ways. Acting as his interpreter was Dr. Vlajic, who invited us to call her Twiggy ("Please do; everyone does").

Before anything else he wanted us to know exactly what had happened a year before. As he related the events, he showed us a new memorial book prepared for the occasion. There were photographs capturing the horror, then for each victim a page with a biography and a picture. As he thumbed through them, he looked like a grandfather mourning dead grandchildren. "I lost many years of my life that night," he murmured, his voice breaking, "but many lost their lives—and I still have mine."

An aide came in; the visitors from Iran had just arrived, and he had to go greet them. I commented to Twiggy how kindly a person he seemed. She nodded. "He is very good."

When he returned, I asked him, "Do you think the Dayton Peace Accords is going to work?"

He shrugged. "Only if all four parts of it are lived up to." Then he enumerated them, throwing out a finger for each one. "First, *return*—of the refugees to their homes. Second, *justice*—the apprehension, trial, and punishment of war criminals ("war-crimers," Twiggy called them). Third, *freedom*—of movement and of the media. Then, and only then, should there be, four, *elections*. Those who signed that protocol—Clinton, Chirac, Kohl, Major—should focus on *all* these points. But they seem to have abandoned the first two."

Then he laughed. "I have always said that elections are like the roof of the house. But now we will be beneath a roof—without a basement!"

We all laughed.

He grew serious again. "If the elections are pushed through now with nothing else accomplished, as some of the participants insist, they will be used to cover and make legitimate the forces that seek to divide and destroy Bosnia-Hercegovina." He smiled sadly. "They will call it democracy, even if we have to jump out the window to vote. They will say, well, you have a free choice: you can jump out the first- or second- or third-floor window!"

I made a note. "Is there anything that gives you hope?"

"I *have* hope! I have always had hope! Even in 1992, when our country was attacked by the fourth largest military power in conventional strength! Bosnia-Hercegovina should have been abolished in four to five weeks. The objective had been the ethnic division of Bosnia." He paused. "But that didn't happen; a thousand years of historic multiculturalism withstood it."

In Tuzla it did not happen at all, and as the war went on, he became 100 percent convinced that Bosnia would survive, and it did.

"What I and my party and all our coalition parties had been telling the people in 1992 is slowly becoming reality. The people are realizing that it is *not* the future of Bosnia, *not* the progress of Bosnia, to be led by national parties into the disintegration of Bosnia-Hercegovina! This is the force, the power that keeps me running and fighting and struggling for true democracy! And we are winning! Today there are many more and quite different Bosnians who share our belief for the future than there were in 1992!"

The mayor loved to tell stories, and I loved to listen. The most amazing was the one he told last. It happened when the corridor across the top of Bosnia had fallen to the JNA. Tuzla was now cut off from Croatia, from which its main supplies had been coming. The army of Bosnia-Hercegovina was poorly organized and even more poorly armed, and the people of Tuzla knew that the army would never be able to defend them. In Croatia, just north of them, the city of Vukovar had been flattened, and Osijek was receiving a terrible bombardment. Tuzla was about to be next and as the aggressors moved their heavy artillery into position, the people braced for the onslaught.

But Mayor Beslagic, meeting with military officers, developed a counter-strategy. If necessary, they would use chlorine from the chemical factory to defend themselves. During World War I, the effect of chlorine gas on the men in the trenches was so horrendous that it was permanently banned from all warfare by the Geneva Convention. As a chemical engineer, the mayor knew its terrible effects and that it was forbidden. But the men who wrote the Geneva Convention would have banned the torture of civilian children and parents before each other's eyes and the use of rape as a weapon of psychosocial destruction—if they could have imagined men ever behaving in such a manner.

So the townspeople positioned huge tanks of chlorine gas directly in the anticipated path of the incoming shells. And then the mayor informed the commander of the aggressors: if you attack us, you will hit these tanks, and then we will *all* die—you, us, and many more besides. Next he informed the worldwide media of the approximate area that would be affected by the release of the gas: it would extend all the way to Zagreb, to Belgrade, and into Hungary.

"I am amazed!" I exclaimed. "I've never heard of a civilian population standing up to an army the size of the JNA! And facing them down! What was their response?"

"Interesting," Selim Beslagic chuckled. "Suddenly the supplies intended for us from Croatia were released. And suddenly the aggressor decided not to press the attack so fiercely on his right flank!"

I looked Selim Beslagic in the eye and asked, "Were you bluffing?"

He just smiled.

I added him to the list.

That evening, a program of commemoration would be held at 8:00 o'clock in the plaza. By 7:30 all the streets leading into the plaza were packed. But Twiggy, who had caught a ride with us, now invited us to the offices of their political organization, which happened to overlook the plaza. Leaning out one of the windows, I could look down several of the side streets, and all I could see was people. The whole city was there. All were watching the plaza, which was bathed in floodlights, not only for the ceremonies but for the video crews that were capturing the event live on national television.

There was a recitation of poetry, a dramatic reading, the singing of a choir—all leading up to the unveiling of a huge memorial that took up the end of one building, facing the plaza. But the most moving moment came when it had grown darker. Apparently everyone had brought candles from home. Now a candle was lighted in the plaza, and the light was passed to other candles, and on and on, proceeding down the dark streets and beyond. Then, their faces aglow with the light of the candles they were holding, the people sang the national hymn of Bosnia-Hercegovina.

Around us, even the seasoned politicos had tears in their eyes, and at that moment I had faith to believe with their mayor: The republic would survive.

SEVENTEEN

GASINCI

According to the road sign, we were to turn right here, head north through the town of Jarmina and on up to Osijek. The large, unwieldy map with which I was wrestling concurred. The only trouble was, on the sign someone had brushed yellow paint over the word Osijek. Well, the map may have been published when Yugoslavia was still Yugoslavia, but roads didn't move. It had been a long day, and there was no sense going another half hour west to Djakovo before turning north, when we could turn north right here. We turned.

The road from Tuzla to the Croatian border had had its share of potholes, but nothing like the one we had driven on the day before. That had been the worst road, bar none, either of us had ever been on. Actually, a relatively good road went from Zenica to Tuzla, but we had been advised to steer clear of Doboj, a Bosnian Serb city where American journalists in a car from Croatia might not be appreciated.

So we had taken the secondary road, which turned out to be a three-hour master class in pothole avoidance. Obviously no funds had been available for road repair for the past five years, and probably not since the collapse of Communism in 1989. Then, too, a lot of fighting had taken place through this area, and many vehicles on the road had come under fire. Each shell had added its crater to the Swiss cheese effect, and the potholes ranged from deep to cavernous. We had become adept at avoiding them, missing twenty-nine out of every thirty. But that thirtieth, usually lurking around a mountain bend, was invariably a deep-dish, sharp-edged, tire-busting teeth-rattler. It was second gear all the way.

But today, we had made good time. In fact, before the border, the only slow-down was at the IFOR checkpoint—a veritable fortress of sandbags, with two enormous tanks facing in opposite directions, each with its long barrel pointing directly at the windshield of any oncoming vehicle. Also present were several beefy armored personnel carriers and a squad of smartly dressed soldiers with a no-nonsense professional attitude. They were totally impressive; no Black Eagles or White Tigers or any other colored animals would ever be tempted to try them.

As we came closer, we saw they were American GIs.

"Any trouble on the road?" a sergeant asked us, as we showed him the car's registration.

"Nope."

"Where are you going?"

"Up to Osijek. Where abouts you from?"

"Dallas. You have a good one now."

"You, too, sergeant."

Luke and I were grinning as we drove away; it was good to hear an American accent.

Then we encountered this day's challenge, also calculated to build one's patience-quota. Like all the other bridges over the Sava River, which separated Bosnia from Croatia, the one on the road from Tuzla to Vinkovici had been blown up during the war. U.S. Army engineers had constructed a temporary metal pontoon bridge, but word had it that only blue-card

(UN-authorized) vehicles could pass, and even some UNHCR vehicles had been turned away.

The alternative was a makeshift car ferry put in service after the bridge went down, which usually had a long wait. We debated trying to talk our way over the IFOR bridge, but decided against it; if it didn't work, we would be out two hours and would still have to take the ferry.

When we arrived at the river, we were the forty-eighth vehicle in line. An average ferry-load was twenty to twenty-two cars with three buses or eighteen-wheelers. It took the ferry about an hour to make a round trip, and took us a little over two to wait in line and then get across. No matter: it was another beautiful, sunny day.

The sky had clouded over by the time we went through Jarmina heading north. We soon noticed that no other cars were ahead of us or behind us; in fact, we had not seen another vehicle since we had left town. Well, here was a checkpoint coming up, with concertina wire (barbed wire in endless loops, with razors instead of barbs) on the road, requiring a driver to slow and negotiate an S through it. On the white guardhouse were large black initials: UN.

But no one was around. The checkpoint was abandoned.

We proceeded more slowly. Obviously, with the arrival of IFOR, patrol and checkpoint duty had passed to them. The sky was becoming more ominous.

We passed a hand-lettered sign by the left side of the road that said "mines," with an arrow pointing into the field. That was okay; we weren't planning on driving in the field.

Another checkpoint loomed ahead. It, too, apparently had been UN, and it, too, was desolate. We slowed even more.

Lightning flashed in the dark sky. "Looks like a storm's brewing," Luke observed, noting the obvious.

Then he slowed almost to a crawl. Up ahead we saw something in the road—a dark mass extending all the way across. When we came a little closer, we saw a huge crater several feet deep, which had spewed out great masses of debris.

"Looks like an antitank mine," I observed, noting the obvious.

"Looks like we'll be turning around," Luke replied. "We don't want to make the next hole." And he shifted into reverse.

"Stay on the pavement," I cautioned needlessly.

We arrived in Osijek around 6:30, four hours later than we'd planned, checked into the hotel, where there was plenty of water, and took a shower. In Tuzla, the water shortage had been severe. It had been turned on only from 6:00 to 8:00, mornings and evenings.

One of our main reasons for coming to Osijek was that I wanted to see a refugee camp. It was arranged for us to see Gasinci, the UN camp about thirty miles outside the city. I had no conception of what one should look like. Obviously it would not resemble a concentration camp; its refugees would be awaiting relocation, not death. But whatever I expected, Gasinci took me by surprise. There were cabins of all sizes on gravel pathways, modern communal buildings, and no litter. Everyone seemed to be outside today, walking, chatting, and getting some sun; it looked almost like a family-style spa. I tried to imagine what it would be like when the weather was cold and rainy and gave up; it was too nice a day.

During the war many tents had been here to handle the flood of people displaced by ethnic cleansing. But now that the war had been over for five months, the population had shrunk back and all could be housed in hard-sided shelters. Three to five months was the average stay in this way station, but the stay could be shortened if a refugee had a relative or friend in a foreign country ready to sponsor him or her. At the other end of the spectrum were the old and sick, who had no sponsors, nor any country that would take them. These were not waiting to go to a new home. They were waiting to die.

Accompanied by a middle-aged, English-speaking woman named Ivanka who worked at the college, we entered a cabin that contained seventeen old people, too sick to be with others. Each had a bunk, some pegs on the wall for their clothing, and a nightstand for their belongings. For most of them that narrow space had been their world for months and would continue to be so for however much longer they lived. Some were coughing, some were asleep, some were sitting on their bunks smoking. Others were just lying down, staring at the ceiling. There was no conversation. No one had anything to say.

The only decoration in the cabin was a wall poster that seemed hideously out of place and mocking: an aerial view of a lush, elegant resort complex on the Italian Riviera, with a sandy beach and sailboats and a tennis court. It was an ad for an Italian bank's credit card.

Ivanka went over to a grizzled old man whom she knew from a previous visit. (The college regularly sent teams of students and staff to Gasinci, to bring some hope and encouragement to these desolate lives.) She sat on his bed and talked with him. At first he was not interested. But as she gently and cheerfully persevered, the old man slowly came to life, and he started crying. She took his hands in hers and spoke intently to him.

I watched as long as I could, then I couldn't take it any longer and had to go outside. Luke did, too.

As the sunlight and warm breeze washed away the sense of hopelessness, I felt guilty for having wanted to leave and for being able to leave. In a few days I would be leaving this tortured land, putting all of this behind me. But I knew I would never forget what I had just experienced.

When she was finished, Ivanka came out and joined us. The old man with whom she had been talking was eighty-two, she told us. He had gone to Germany to be with his son, who was forty-four and in a refugee camp there. But his son, unable to care for him, had sent him back here. When he thought about it, it made him cry.

But Ivanka had said to him, "Look at all these burdens you have! God doesn't give those to weak people! He gave them to you, because you are strong enough to carry them!" And at that he had smiled at her and become peaceful in his heart.

I added Ivanka to the list.

EIGHTEEN

DR. K

Osijek — Celebrating the eight-hundredth anniversary of its present name, Osijek (In Roman times called Mursa) had grown along the south bank of the River Drava. Alongside this smooth, deep river, at the heart of the oldest part of the city, ran a broad esplanade with many outdoor cafés. Because the weather was warm, and optimism was returning along with people on holiday, they would be filled tonight, provided it didn't rain. But given the ominous overcast, dropping temperature, and rising wind, that was a large proviso.

Adjacent to the esplanade was a manmade inlet, a place for pleasure craft to park if their owners wanted to linger a few hours or perhaps spend the night ashore. It was empty now, but before the war, when people had the time and the money and chose to spend it cruising the river, the inlet had been quite full. Cruising west from Osijek, you encountered mostly farmland, but a few miles to the east, the Drava flowed into the Danube. From there you could go southeast to Belgrade or north to Budapest and Vienna.

If you did go south, the first city en route would be Osijek's sister, Vukovar—a little older, and perhaps once the more beautiful, though Osijek's suitors would never agree. Archeologically, Vukovar was definitely more significant.

Before the war, a stone dove was unearthed there that experts estimated to be at least three thousand years old. The Vukovar Dove became widely known as a symbol of the new peace—a poignantly ironic symbol considering Vukovar had been completely destroyed by the war. It had the misfortune of being right next to the Serbian border and was the aggressors' first major target when they launched their invasion. Caught by surprise, the city was unable to put up an adequate defense. But the resistance it did mount was stiff enough for the aggressors to make an example of the city. They leveled it and pounded it into rubble, and then they kept on pounding it, even though all they were doing was bouncing bricks. Trying to describe what had been done to Vukovar, the media coined a new word: urbanicide.

By another unplanned coincidence, we had arrived in Osijek at the opening of a week-long remembrance known as the Days of Vukovar, during which Osijek (joined via live television by all of Croatia) would commemorate its sister city. What was left of Vukovar was still in the 9.4 percent of territory yet to be returned to Croatia, but under the terms of the Dayton Peace Accords, before the end of the year the remains of the city were to be given back to its citizens.

One of the reasons we had come to Osijek was to see Dr. Peter Kuzmic, founding director of both the Evangelical Theological Seminary and Agape. Peter was one of the key peacemakers. He was also (for reasons we would shortly discover) among the handful of guests invited to the opening ceremony of the Days of Vukovar—a private reception by the mayor of Osijek for the mayor of Vukovar. Peter had taken us to a private showing of a photographic exhibition of Vukovar before and after, and now he was giving us a tour of the city he loved.

Reminiscent in feel of Vienna, Osijek had acres of parks

and numerous historic facades. Peter showed us the new National Opera House, whose restoration had recently been completed and was an absolute gem, and the ancient, half-buried Roman stables across the river; apparently the patricians of Caesar's time had also discovered the tranquil pleasures of this region. But my favorite aspect of Osijek was the picturesque trolley whose track did not run down the middle of the avenue as one might expect, but on the grassy strip between the sidewalk and the street, which gave it an irresistible charm.

As we drove and walked about, Peter had been filling us in on what had happened during the siege of Osijek at the beginning of the war. My estimate of the seemingly limitless supply of JNA munitions had not been an exaggeration: in eight months an incredible 150,000 shells had rained down on the city, destroying some 24,000 homes and civic buildings—one out of every three. But the worst statistic was the one that prefigured Srebrenica: 1,800 men had been taken captive, led away, and never seen again.

As Peter spoke, certain things he said indicated to me that he had played a personal role in the events of that siege. I probed, and it turned out he had, indeed. Out came my ubiquitous microrecorder, and we repaired to one of the outdoor cafés for cappuccino. We had the place to ourselves. The wind was whipping the tablecloths; a storm was definitely on the way.

Peter Kuzmic was middle-aged and of middle height and weight. But there was nothing middling about his fine Balkan mustache, or the knowing twinkle in his eye. His mind was far-ranging and ever-alert, and his wit was quick. Were I a student at Gordon-Conwell Theological Seminary north of Boston, where he was professor of Foreign Missions, I would count myself fortunate to be in one of his courses. I had first heard of him years before; I had even written about him in the last chapter of David du Plessis's last book. He was the pastor who had taken David to Medjugorje.

Peter had a unique arrangement with Gordon-Conwell that enabled him to spend half his time based in Osijek, and he had been here with his wife and three daughters when the war came to this city. Like everyone else, he had not believed that it would spread or intensify. When the first shells started falling in his neighborhood shortly after midnight, he was shocked. This could not be happening! But it was, and their house had no basement. In the midst of the bombardment, they ran across the street to take shelter in the basement of a neighbor.

Night after night the bombardment continued, until one night a grenade landed so near that only a wall separated them from it. The explosion with its blinding white flash and concussion was stupendous. His younger daughter, Petra, was traumatized (and four years later still had trouble sleeping). He evacuated his family and the seminary to neighboring Slovenia from which he came originally. They set up school right on the Hungarian border, so they would be safe from air attack[13] (the aggressors would not risk violating Hungarian airspace).

One of their number refused to leave: Chris Marshall from Seattle, who had taught English in their school for years. In the hospital recovering from a bicycle accident when they came to collect her, Chris had refused to leave the city, in spite of the orders from the American Embassy and State Department that all Americans were to leave the war zone immediately. Her reply: "I have higher orders. They

---

[13] This was before NATO's "you fly, you die" edict grounded the aggressors' bombers.

come from the Lord of Hosts." And so she stayed, feeding refugees, helping the elderly, and taking Serb families into her home to protect them from vengeful Croats. As she went about ministering to these people, she earned a wry but fitting nickname: "the evangelical Mother Teresa of Osijek."

Peter and his family were back in the States on November 18, 1991, when he received the news that Vukovar had fallen. Soon he received an urgent cable from Cardinal Kuharic:

> HELP US [STOP] OUR THREE FRANCIS-
> CANS FROM VUKOVAR HAVE BEEN TAKEN
> CAPTIVE [STOP] WE DON'T KNOW WHERE,
> OR IF THEY ARE ALIVE [STOP] WE FEAR
> THEY HAVE BEEN BADLY BEATEN AND MAY
> BE DEAD [STOP]

Peter had met Senator Bob Dole and his wife Elizabeth, whose nephew attended Gordon-Conwell. He immediately sent a fax to Elizabeth, who was then secretary of housing and development under President Bush, and another to the Senate Majority Leader. He quickly received faxes back, assuring him that they would do everything they could and that they *would* find the Franciscans. In two weeks, the three priests were released. As was feared, they had been horribly beaten, but they were alive.

Meanwhile, the aggressors had now turned their full attention on Osijek. In a hurry to take the city and reach the oil fields just beyond, they surrounded Osijek on three sides, bringing their heaviest artillery to bear. But unlike Vukovar, here the Territorial Defense Force had had a chance to dig in. They were determined that Osijek would not share the fate of Vukovar.

Inside the cordon there was panic. People were fleeing by the thousands. The railroad station was a mob scene. Only one road remained open—a narrow, two-lane affair jammed with cars and people and under constant bombardment. In less than a month, the population of this city shrank from 150,000 to 19,000. The aggressors were doing their utmost to close the noose. They had not succeeded, but for those still inside, the situation was desperate and growing critical. Food and medical supplies were gone, and they were beginning to starve.

Peter received a phone call from a longtime friend and academic colleague, Professor Kramaric, Osijek's first freely elected mayor after the fall of Communism. He told Peter of the lack of food and help and supplies at the hospital, and of other shortages. He concluded by pleading, "Peter, is there *anything* you can do?"

Peter said he didn't know, but he was going to do everything he possibly could. He started by going to the president of Gordon-Conwell and telling him that he had to return to Osijek, immediately.

"Are you crazy?"

"I have to."

By now the president knew Peter well enough to know that, once his mind was made up, there was no point arguing with him. "All right, but leave your family here. We'll look after them."

In Zagreb, he went to see Cardinal Kuharic, who expressed his gratitude for what Peter had done to effect the release of the Franciscans. He told the cardinal he was going into Osijek.

"Don't be crazy!" the cardinal admonished him. "Nobody can get in there now. There's just that little road, and they're attacking it and shelling it day and night."

He went to see an old church friend of his and told him of his plan. "That's crazy!" said his friend. "You're throwing your life away!"

"I'm not," Peter replied, "not when I follow the Lord and the words of His Spirit." For he had a strong inner conviction that this was what God wanted him to do.

His last call was on Ivan Vekic, the Croatian Minister of the Interior who had married the daughter of church friends of his.

"It's very dangerous to go there," the minister said, repeating what everyone else had told him. Then he shook his head and smiled. "But I know you people of faith; you have this crazy courage. Well, since you're obviously going anyway, let me give you some instructions."

The minister asked two military experts to advise Peter and some former students who had volunteered to go with him. Their briefing was short and not sweet: "Go in two cars, and keep a good distance apart. If they attack from the air, and that's still possible, the moment you hear or see them, *stop*! Get out of the car on both sides and spread out *fast* into the fields or corn or whatever. If they're diving on you, they have only a split second to pick their target. If you stay in clusters, it's too easy for them."

The other man shook his head. "Your problem's not going to be from the air. It's going to be artillery. They're using it to interdict the road. If they start shelling you, just floor the pedal and keep it floored! Go as fast as your cars can carry you!"

Peter looked around at his young friends. "All right, you've heard what's in store. If any of you wants to drop out, it's all right." None did.

Peter would drive the lead car, a Citroen 16DX. At the wheel of the second car, a Volkswagen Golf, was a young

Baptist pastor who had been a former student. It fell to Peter to decide whether to make the run at night or in broad daylight. At night, the gunners would have more difficulty seeing them. But it would also be harder for them to see potholes and other road hazards, and after all the shelling the surface was undoubtedly in terrible shape by now. Sneaking through without lights was out of the question; the road was too closely monitored. In the end he decided on daylight: if they were going to be doing top-speed driving, they had better be able to see where they were going. There was not much point in being killed in a car crash, before they even reached the city.

At that point in his story, the heavens began to shell us with rain. The first fat drops fell, interrupting our conversation, and we scampered to get under cover. When we were settled, Peter resumed.

They would go at first light, when the gunners would be either dead tired at the end of their watch or still half asleep as they came on duty. They drove as close as they could, and then, taking a deep breath, they hit the accelerator and started their run. The gunners became all too wide awake and soon began tracking them. Peter, driving the lead car, gunned the engine. Swerving around potholes, they were soon flying down the road at triple the speed limit. But so were the explosions, which were gaining on them.

"How fast are we going?" Peter called to his young comrade.

"It looks like—160 kilometers!"

"That's ridiculous! This car can't go that fast!"

"Well, it is now!"

"Are you praying?"

"Dr. K, I never stopped!"

Both cars made it.

Peter went first to the hospital. As in other bombardments, the hospital was one of the first targets. Because the upper floors were destroyed, all action was in the basement. As he watched, doctors operated on the constant stream of wounded. They had to operate without anesthesia, for there was none left. The patients, knowing that the doctors and nurses were doing their best, tried not to cry out. But they couldn't help it. Peter sobbed.

But he knew what he must do now. He saw the head of the hospital, the mayor, and others, writing down their greatest needs. And then it was time to run the gauntlet again. This time the closest he came to his eternal reward happened before they even left the city. It was growing dark, and he was driving on Strossmeyer Street just crossing an intersection when a streak of white lightning flashed in front of his windshield and exploded against the wall of the building next to him. Momentarily blinded by the burst of light and rocked by the concussion, he was unscathed. And miraculously so was the car. It still ran, and he could still drive it as fast as it could go.

He made it through without incident. When he arrived in Zagreb, he went to see Father Jurak, a Catholic pastor who was an old friend. When Peter had been an evangelical pastor in Zagreb, they used to hold joint ecumenical services in Father Jurak's church. He went to his friend now, because by this time Zagreb had 100,000 refugees, and Father Jurak's church had been given the responsibility of caring for a large number of them, feeding them through the auspices of the Catholic relief agency, Caritas.

The old friends hugged, and when he explained his mission, Father Jurak took him outside. It was December now and snowing. Around the church a long queue of people stood patiently in line for food, shivering, hunched over against the cold. They would stamp their feet to keep their circulation going, their breath making puffs in the icy air. Many were old people with little plastic bags, hoping to get some yogurt or bread for their grandchildren. Father Jurak shook his head. "I have seven thousand and I have food for only two hundred." And with that he started to cry.

Peter's mission now became the most important of his life. Finding a friend who would let him use his home phone, he spent all night on the phone, calling friends in America, in Germany, in England, and a dozen other countries. He had friends all over the world, and while he had done favors for many, he had never asked them for help before. Not like this. But lives were at stake, more than anyone could imagine. "Listen," he would say, "if you believe in God, as I know you do, then you must do something. Christians cannot be indifferent when you see so much pain and suffering. We need your help, now! Get on the radio, put it in newspapers, ask laypeople in your church to help. Set up storage depots, trucks for shipment. But don't put it off; there is no time left. They are out of food *right now*!"

The people Peter called knew him. They knew that he never exaggerated. They promised help, as fast as they could send it. The Body of Christ was responding to a hurt member.

The next night he called a meeting of pastors and church leaders in Zagreb. He had hardly slept for days, but he seemed to have an infusion of mental and physical energy. "The food *is* coming," he told them. "In a few days the first trucks from Germany will be arriving. We need to get ready. We need to set up an organization with good accountability structures, efficient distribution, and fast coordination, so that the most needy will get the help first."

And that was how Agape was born.

As if on cue, torrential rain now swept in under the

awning, and we had to dash for the car. Later, as Luke and I drove him back to the seminary, I asked him, "It's a spiritual battleground here, isn't it?"

He nodded. "The kingdom of light is in conflict with the kingdom of darkness here, and we hope that the light will carry the victory. Keep in mind: God loves Bosnia and the Bosnian people. And His purposes *will* be established."

"Then you're hopeful?"

"Of course!" He paused. "You know what hope is? Hope is faith turned toward the future."

We had reached the seminary, but he hesitated before getting out. "There is a quote by St. Augustine, which I thought of often during the war: 'Hope has two daughters—anger and courage. Anger about the ways things are, and courage to change them.'"

He opened the door, then turned back. "And here is one more: I can't remember where I heard it, and I probably have the words wrong, but: 'Hope is the ability to hear the music of the future; faith is the courage to dance to it in the present.'"

And with his name, I closed the list.

NINETEEN

NOT A PRETTY ROAD

Our mission accomplished, we were heading south in the driving rain, trying to make it from Osijek to Medjugorje in a single day. We had left before dawn and crossed on the ferry in good time. (Because our car was small, we were allowed to go ahead of the forty-seven freight trucks that had been waiting for hours.) The road south to Tuzla had been flat and straight, and now we were on the stretch to Sarajevo. It had been raining heavily since we started, and the mountain potholes were treacherous; filled with water, we had no idea how deep they were. Still, we were making good time. Luke was driving this stretch while I navigated. I checked my watch; it was just past 1:00 P.M. By suppertime, we should make the new convent where we would be Sister Janja's guests, *nema problema*.

We were up in the mountains again and came around a corner to see something large and brown like a big toad parked crosswise in the road ahead of us. It was an IFOR armored personnel carrier (APC), in front of which stood two soldiers in burgundy berets—Italian *caribinieri*. They signaled us to stop.

"What's the problem?" I asked, hoping one of them understood English.

"Bridge out. You turn round; go back to Olovo. Take road to Vares."

This was not exactly a surprise. At the last IFOR checkpoint, we had been warned that the bridge on the main road from Tuzla to Sarajevo was under reconstruction. We were to take the detour at Olovo that ran east and then south through Vares. Well, we had obviously missed that detour; in fact, we had missed Olovo—sailed right through it without noticing. Bosnians were not much for detour signs, or any other directional information, for that matter; if you didn't know where you were going, you shouldn't be going.

I showed our map to the soldier who could speak a little English and asked him where we were. He pointed to an intersection about twenty miles below Olovo. "So we must go back?" I asked him.

He nodded. "Or," he shrugged, "go there." He gestured to a little road that went off to the right and shook his head. "Is not a pretty road."

"Does it go to Vares?"

"Si, *but is not a pretty road!*" He said it with emphasis this time; I had obviously not been paying attention.

Luke and I had a consultation. By the time we got all the way back up to Olovo, it would be 1:45. On the other hand, if we took this side road . . . it wasn't on the map, but it *was* paved, and the IFOR guy did say it went to Vares. So what if it wasn't pretty; by this time, we had certainly seen ugly. It couldn't be any worse than that road from Zenica to Tuzla. We decided to take it.

The road went across a field and around a bend, and now two guys standing in the road in camies waved us down. They were bareheaded, not more than eighteen or nineteen, and their fatigues didn't match. Paramilitaries? Or just a couple of kids having some fun with the car from

Croatia? They didn't speak English, but they made it clear we were supposed to turn around. When we didn't respond right away, they gestured ahead of us and shouted, "*Mina! Mina!*" So there were mines up ahead; well, if we stayed on the pavement. . . .

"They don't look like IFOR to me," I whispered to Luke at the wheel. "I don't trust them."

"Yeah, and those IFOR guys back at the APC said we could get through this way."

We went ahead. After about two miles the pavement quit, and we were on a dirt road that was sometimes little more than a track, with many potholes. We seldom shifted to second gear, and never third. The road went through rolling farmland which, had the sun been out, would have been quite pretty, even if the road wasn't. As it was, with all the rain and fog, the day had a decidedly gloomy cast to it.

It soon became apparent that this terrain had been more heavily fought over than any rural territory we had been through. Deep trenches were cut across the road and hastily filled in, and every house had been killed. We saw no one, nor did we see any farm animals or any planted crops—nothing. The afternoon was definitely becoming eerie.

We climbed steadily, and after a while there were no more houses, just old trees that increasingly became firs as we went higher. I took another look at the map. Where we were, there was *nothing* for many miles in any direction. All I could tell was that we were in the Cemerno Mountains, somewhere north of Sarajevo.

Then our dirt road ran into another dirt road and stopped. There was no sign, no way of telling whether we should go left or right. There was no sun to tell which direction was which, and the road we had been on had made so many twists and turns, we were completely disoriented. The one thing that did not occur to either of us was that we ought to go back. We had now spent forty-five minutes on this road, and that was too much of an investment to throw away. Besides, we must be getting *somewhere*.

But which way to go? We decided to pray and not proceed until we were in agreement as to which way we should go. We went left. The road climbed higher. We were in virgin timber now, very tall, very old, making the day very dark. The rain came harder, and the road got rougher, with jagged rocks sticking out of it. Second gear was a distant memory. Well, the *caribinieri* was right: it was definitely not a pretty road.

After two and a half hours, we had made more than twenty direction decisions, and we were both growing extremely tired of picking our way along. At that moment I had the distinct impression of God's grace on us, in spite of everything. I mentioned it to Luke who said it was a good thing; we could use it.

It must have been grace that kept us from being fearful, because we were now hopelessly lost. Of course, if anyone had said that to us then, we would have vehemently denied it. But there was no way we could have found our way back out of there; there were simply too many turns. When spelunkers explore new caves, they are meticulously careful to mark the beginning of each tunnel with colored chalk. It hadn't occurred to us to keep track of which way we were going. We just prayed and went.

It got to be 4:00 o'clock. We had been wandering in this wilderness for three hours, during which time we had covered only 35 miles. Plus, it was beginning to get really dark, and in another couple of hours would be night. And we had less than a quarter of a tank of gas left—not enough to get back the way we had come, even if we knew which way that was.

And yet still we were not scared—which was in no way to our credit; the poor souls who lost their lives on Everest about the same time were not scared, either, until the very end. They had not realized how serious was the trouble they were in, until after it was too late to do anything about it. The thought did cross my mind: What would we do if we slid on the mud, went into a ditch, and got really stuck, or blew a tire on one of those rocks, or broke a fuel line like Father Svet did when he was on a road like this one. But I didn't dwell on it; I sensed God was with us, even if we didn't know where we were.

One good thing: we were alongside a creek, heading downstream, and the last four turn-decisions had kept us beside that stream. I knew that in mountain-climbing, if one was ever completely lost and came across running water, one followed it downstream and never left it; eventually it would lead to civilization.

Another good thing: due to the rain, we could see tire tracks. Some cars had passed that way today, because it hadn't rained much in the north in about eight days.

Then we came to a turn where we couldn't agree. If we turned right, which I wanted to do, we stayed with the stream. If we turned left, which Luke wanted to do, we would follow more fresh tracks.

We sat and waited. Finally, I said, "Okay, we'll go your way. We can always come back if it's wrong."

We went left and soon started climbing again. This had to be wrong, I thought; we're going back up the mountain we just came down. I was on the verge of pointing this out and suggesting that we reverse course, when I noticed something moving—a large shape in the field to our left, ambling up into the tree line, taking its time.

It was a great brown bear.

We rolled up our windows, which is what one does in Yellowstone when a bear is in the vicinity. But this one was so much bigger than those, it made the memory of them seem almost cuddly by comparison. I had never seen a grizzly, but I couldn't imagine its being any larger than this bear.

That was when I finally realized just how deeply into this mountain wilderness we truly were. A *bear* was over there! So used to being alone and unchallenged, it was utterly disinterested in our presence.

We drove on and came to another T and prayed and turned left.

Something else was moving up ahead, along the left side of the road. It was another animal, not in the bear class, walking on all fours by the side of the road, heading in the same direction we were going. From the rear it looked to be about the size of a big collie, with wiry gray fur and a short gray patch of a tail. Its head was hanging down, so we couldn't see it, but its hindquarters seemed unnaturally thin, and we caught a glimpse of ribs along its right flank. It had not eaten in a long time.

"What is it?" asked Luke.

"Beats me." Why hadn't it heard us and gotten out of there? "Honk at it."

Luke tapped the horn.

Instead of bolting into the bush, it just kept plodding along.

When we had closed to within ten yards, Luke honked again.

No response.

Then, just as we were almost on top of it, it suddenly became aware of us, and startled, it scrabbled across the road.

As Luke braked, it turned a wide, fear-filled eye toward us.

It was a wild boar. But it was unlike anything we had ever seen. The head, too big for the body, was horribly misshapen. There was no face; where the snout and jaws should have been, it seemed to be all hollowed out. And in the hollow was nothing but darkness.

It looked like a creature from hell.

"Jesus!" I shouted, meaning it, as it disappeared into the bush. We were both shaken.

I did not want to think about spending the night in our car or of walking out of there in the morning—whichever way "out" was.

Around the next bend Luke braked again. There, filling the road in front of us, was a huge logging truck, with a crew of three loggers using a cherry-picking crane to load dressed-out timber on the back of it. We were saved.

The loggers were astonished to see our little car up there—dumbfounded when they realized it contained two lost Americans. We didn't know if they were Serbs or Muslims or Croats, and could not care less. They were alive, and they didn't live in the woods.

They made it clear that we should wait until they were finished, then we could follow them out. We waited.

I could not take my mind off that boar, and gradually I figured out what had happened to him. This area had been a battlefield. Whenever the aggressors withdrew from an area, they left mines and booby traps behind, so that no one could use it. That poor animal had set off one of those devices. It had blown off his face, so that he could not eat. He was starving to death. It was not that his head was too big for his body; his body had shrunk too small for his head. Also, his hearing must have been destroyed by the blast, which was why he hadn't heard us. He must be exhausted and in terrible pain, and in another day or two he would die.

It was 9:40 when we arrived in Medjugorje. We were Sister Janja's guests at the new convent there, and though we were four hours late and the phones were out when we tried to call them from the road, they had kept supper warm for us. I could not remember anything ever tasting so good.

The next morning, as I was having an early coffee, I thought about the day before. Obviously we had been foolish to go off the map to save a little time. But what else was there in it?

What came to me was that it was the defining as well as the concluding experience of this pilgrimage. A spiritual battle was going on for the soul of Bosnia, and only a spiritual solution was going to bring a happy ending. People still believed that with enough time and goodwill, they could bring an end to the cycle of hatred. But no amount of time was enough. And goodwill was little more than a sentiment on Christmas cards. People could not heal Bosnia.

God could. But humanity would have to ask Him; He would not do it without being asked. And without His intervention, the darkness would only spread and go deeper.

In the mountain wilderness, Luke and I were totally lost—only we weren't, not really. What kept us from becoming a pair of stupid, senseless fatalities was that we had trusted God. And through an incredibly circuitous route He had led us to that logging crew, the one certain way of getting out of there.

Bosnia was, in a sense, in a similar situation: she was wandering in a wilderness, low on gas, with daylight running out. She could not go back; she could only go forward. But which way? God could show her, but she would have to ask Him. Without God, she was lost and would soon be a stupid, senseless fatality.

Right now she was looking to her warmakers for leadership. But if she were to look to her peacemakers, they just might be able to show her the way out.

EPILOGUE

The next morning, our last in Bosnia, I went to the English Mass. One of the priests concelebrating was an American, whose party had experienced a death three days before. An ailing old woman had expired on Mount Krizevac. Her son had been with her and was now taking her body home. But on the morning before they had gone to the mountain, the pilgrims on her tour had given her a gift: a wooden cross which they all had signed.

The priest asked the congregation if, as a sort of memorial, they might sing "The Old Rugged Cross." I was surprised that he had requested an old evangelical hymn—and even more surprised when it turned out to be in the paperback English hymnals distributed for the service.

We started to sing, and I found the simple old hymn more powerful than I ever remembered. When it came to the part in the chorus that said, "Till my trophies at last I lay down; I will cling to the old rugged cross. . . ," I could no longer see the page, for the tears.

I surrendered.